The Story of My S‹

How to survive trauma and overcome anore

First written in 2016 with blog po:

Revised edition May 2019.

By Nell Flowers / Lena Carter.

For Mum and Dad.

Contents

Part One

"What would you write if you weren't afraid? Write that."

DBC Pierre

It is time. It is time to write and say it all. This is a message to myself and to whoever needs to know. For almost forty years, I have been hiding from myself. From my self.

But I need to do this now.

Because some days, even now, I still feel like I don't want to live.

Because I still wake up anxious on a daily basis.

Because deep down I have a sense that I don't deserve to be here.

Because I am too often irritable and unkind to those I love the most.

Because there are days when I consider leaving my children with their father so that they won't have to live with my erratic, difficult, damaging behaviour.

Because I can see the ways in which I behave and feel about myself starting to appear in my daughter.

Because I still can't go a day without exercising.

Because I push myself beyond tiredness and live with an almost constant sense of exhaustion.

Because I am a workaholic.

Because I still get stressed if someone offers me a biscuit with a cup of tea.

Because I don't eat lunch whenever possible as it makes me feel better.

Because I cannot ever rest. Because nothing is ever good enough. The house is not clean enough, we never have enough money, I never have enough friends, my work is never done well enough.

I am not enough.

Because my husband said to me the other day that I go to sleep and wake up talking about work. And he feels left out.

Because it is painful and hurtful to admit to those you love and who share your world that you are not happy in that world.

I need to stop hurting. Hurting myself and hurting others.

Most of the time I do well at hiding the truth. And I do count my blessings and feel grateful. I am, on paper, a huge success. I do and have it all. I am a senior manager. I am married to a truly wonderful man; I have found my 'other half'. I have two incredible children. I write a blog about wellbeing which gets positive feedback and praise for my 'insight and honesty'.

I tweet all the right quotes and share all the right inspirational ideas on Facebook.

I have trained as a therapist and been in therapy and counselling. I have read endlessly about mindfulness, psychology, brain development, eating disorders and mental health. I know as much as there is for a non-expert to know about recent research into attachment, trauma and behaviour.

I know that a tendency to overwork and be driven are easy addictions to continue with in our driven society. Hard work is a GOOD thing; workaholism is one of those addictions that is secretly ok because it is about 'achieving'. As is an addiction to exercise. You don't get the same criticism for being addicted to work or exercise as you do for being addicted to alcohol or cocaine.

But although I know this, I continue with the ways of behaving that I have developed over years.

My mantra, to the people that I work with, is that you must work on knowing and liking your self above all else. You are the only person guaranteed to walk alongside you until the end of your days and if you get that relationship right, others will be easy.

Until this moment, I have talked that talk and not been able to walk that walk.

But no more.

Until now I have hidden the truth because I have feared that there is no solution. That no one can help me feel better. That I am just a freak, unfixable, a tragic combination of genes, maybe autistic or bipolar or just mentally ill. A brain or a mind gone wrong and never to be made right.

But a conversation last week made me realise that it is in my control to make it right. There is a simple part of the puzzle that needs to be fitted before I can move on.

Some bad things happened to me once. On the scale of it, they weren't really bad things and other people might have experienced them and not reacted as I did. But for me, they were traumatic and resulted in me developing ways of trying to protect myself against trauma in the future.

Ways of thinking, ways of behaving, ways of being.

Over the years, those ways of behaving have become engrained and they are hard to let go of.

But hard is not impossible.

Life is not perfect. Bad things happen and we can't always control events around us. There are good feelings as well as bad. But we can have control over our thoughts and our actions if we understand, deeply, who we are and why we have behaved in certain ways in the past.

This is my story.

It is based on a number of diary entries and memories.

The diary entries are reproduced and re-typed exactly as they were hand-written, except where I have altered things to preserve anonymity. I admit to cringing at many of them but they were and therefore are part of me. Brené Brown has written about the need for us to live with shame and vulnerability and in telling this story I make myself vulnerable.

I am telling this story to help me understand it and to help me move on. And why am I telling you? Because maybe, just maybe, I can help you too. You aren't me and you will have your own story to tell. But perhaps in reading my story you will gain some hope. We can be broken and we can be fixed again. People will hurt us but we can stop hurting. We can survive but we can do more than survive; we can thrive.

Once you have read my story, write your own. And get others to write theirs. Don't let them sit on the hurt for 40 years.

There are moments in this story where it is clear that I made huge strides forward in my understanding and life. But there is also a repetition of key themes; in many ways this leads me to a sense of frustration as to why I did not get further sooner. The same positive things said, the same promises to do what was needed but then these promises broken and shown to be shallow words. Talking the talk but not really believing what I was saying or walking the walk. Failing to admit to an underlying truth so obvious yet so difficult to acknowledge. The simplest thing which has resulted in huge long term complication and confusion.

Until now I have refused to face up to the thing that has blocked the sun. And I have failed to put to rest my sense of not being worthy of all the sun's light and warmth.

It is the ultimate source of my shame and the hardest truth to tell.

Part Two

Inspiration

An 'inner story' is exactly what it says it is – a story. It is a collection of connected thoughts in your mind that are interwoven to create a narrative about you and what it means to be you. However, an inner story is not just a story that you write and tell. It is also a story that you listen to, act upon and live. As it is your story you can edit it and change it if you want to and whenever you want to. But first of all you need to know it so that you can establish whether it is working for you. If you do not know your inner story you can sleepwalk through your life, giving permission for anything at all to happen unchecked inside your mind.

Inner Story. Understand your Mind. Change your World. Dr Tim O' Brien.

Words - spoken or written- are what connect us to the world, and so speaking about it to people, and writing about this stuff, helps connect us to each other, and to our true selves.

Reasons to Stay Alive. Matt Haig

Friends, family or therapists can provide advice and support, but in the end it comes down to you as an individual making that choice to keep trying, no matter what. Surround yourself with kind people, by all means, and treat others well. But remember that no-one else's love and care can replace you loving and caring for yourself. We all go wrong sometimes, we get hurt and we hurt others. But we also have the capacity to start afresh, every morning if need be. Belief in oneself, compassion for others, and a generous helping of optimism can work wonders. When things seem hopeless, when there's nothing to look forward to, make something up- write a list, formulate a plan, work towards a dream, plan a journey, start a conversation. Invent your reason to keep going.

Letting Go. Emma Woolf

Harry, there is never a perfect answer in this messy emotional world. Perfection is beyond the reach of humankind, beyond the reach of magic. In every shining moment of happiness is that drop of poison; the knowledge that pain will come again. Be honest to those you love, show your pain. To suffer is as human as to breathe.

Albus Percival Wulfric Brian Dumbledore.

Harry Potter and the Cursed Child. JK Rowling, John Tiffany and Jack Thorne.

Part Three

<u>The last 16 years.</u>

So much absolutely wonderful and magical stuff has happened.

I met the right man and discovered that I could be loved and share my life with someone else. We had great adventures; trekking in the Far East, adventuring across Europe and Canada, camping, canoeing, skiing.

My strange fears and obsessions were mainly kept in check; enough exercise meant that I could eat with relatively little guilt.

This man helped me to start to enjoy food again, to stop seeing it as an enemy. To eat with someone else and feel relaxed about it.

Irrational fears have generally been overruled by his wise words.

We married and I gave birth to two amazing, precious children. Given my history, the very fact that this happened easily is nothing short of a miracle.

We have moved around the country several times and generally made a 'success' of whatever we have done. We have also made mistakes and learned from them.

We have had the most satisfying, fulfilling times watching our children grow. We have remembered and relived the joy, freedom and spontaneity of childhood. We have laughed, loved, played and struggled.

I have had success in my career.

But I still, on occasions, feel like this, which I wrote just last December, three days before Christmas:

I feel:
I can't do it any more because I'm too broken and can't ever be fixed.
I know:
I can and I'm not and things can be broken and still go on working.
I feel:
I have no friends.
I know:
I do have good friends.
I feel:
Worthless.
I know:
I have worth and can offer a lot.
I feel:
Everything is wrong.
I know:
Lots of things are right.

I feel:

Disgust.
I know:
I am not disgusting.
I feel:
No-one understands me.
I know:
No-one ever can fully understand me but I can understand myself.
I feel:
Like the worst spouse and parent in the world.
I know:
I am a good spouse and parent.
I feel:
Like I don't want to be here.
I know:
That I do want to be here.
I feel:
Exhausted.
I know:
That I am exhausted but can get through it.
I feel:
Like I have to keep going.
I know:
That I have to rest.
I feel:
Sad
I know:
I have been and can be happy.

And I also know I can feel joyous, excited, loving, spontaneous and proud.

What I know will get me through and help me to fight the feelings when they visit.

Let this serve to remind me....

#hopefor2016

There has been so much joy, magic and genuine happiness. Happiness which for a time I believed would never be mine.

Part Four

My early working life.

Diary extract

9th January 1994

I feared all weekend that I would have put on lots of weight because I haven't run since Wednesday however after running on Sunday evening my weight hasn't gone up. I've eaten sporadically (six slices of bread and butter, lots of apples, some crisps, 3 bacardis, 3 vodkas, one banana, one carrot, one chocolate biscuit) but it hasn't caused catastrophe and I'm still alive. I am stressed out because I haven't done any yoga or situps today.

I am a horrific friend. I am cold to K and moody and all I seem to do is bring her down. I am sure she wants me to move out.

Memories

I remember this time well. I was depressed and struggled to adjust to a new lifestyle, colleagues and expectations after university. I went to the doctor and was prescribed anti-depressants which I never took.

I had counselling and worked my way through a book of Cognitive Behavioural Therapy to try and manage my low mood and negative thinking. I wrote screeds and screeds of 'self-analysis' and attempted to convert feelings of sadness, anxiety and fear into positivity and optimism. But I felt sad and detached from life.

I was a cold and unpleasant person to be around and I was very difficult to live with; I feel bad to this day that I treated my housemate of the time as I did.

Only at work did I continue to 'succeed'. A brilliant practitioner and astonishingly competent for one so new to the profession. At the end of my first year of work I had to go through an in-depth medical in order to be given a permanent contract in my second post, having ticked a box to say that I had suffer from depression/anxiety within the previous five years. A few days of utter panic and despair, fearing that I would never be free of my 'guilty past'. But I managed to convince them of my sanity.

On the outside, I had everything through the years that followed. I had a good series of jobs and was promoted quickly. I had a string of relationships but nothing that lasted more than 6 months and most lasting significantly less. Several were utterly inappropriate and put me at risk. Alcohol played a big part in this but in the ladette culture of the nineties, this was de rigeur.

Of course the alcohol I drank had to be maximum impact for minimum calories and so my tipple of choice was a double vodka on the rocks.

My life in many ways resembled that of Bridget Jones only with more self-control over food.

I was vegetarian and rarely ate in front of others when it could be avoided. When sharing a house with other friends for three years, my diet consisted mainly of jacket potatoes, cottage cheese, salad and fruit.

I exercised a lot and was nearly sent over the edge when I had to stop running due to injury.

After a few years I trained, alongside doing my job to be a therapist.

I went into therapy. Both individual, which I liked, and group therapy, which I loathed and never opened up in. I came a reasonably long way in understanding my fears. Towards the end of individual therapy, my therapist told me that I'd done a great job but that I could not be helped any further unless I was honest about what had hurt me.

He knew.

I began to open up to some extent; with him and with friends whom I had learnt to love and trust. I started to be honest about the difficulties I had faced and continued to face but never really admitted that I needed to do more or go further into looking at my thinking and behaviours.

Part Five

<u>The university years.</u>

Memories

I went to university a shadow of the girl I had been when I had applied to go.

It was a struggle but somehow I survived it. In my first year I was desperately sad and homesick.

Diary extract

February 1989

I feel as though I am being dragged through a dark tunnel with something totally frightening at the end and there is no escape. I just want to stop and curl up in a ball and not think but I can't. Because my thoughts are controlling everything. It hurts so much inside and I'm so scared but at the same time I want to tell myself to snap out of it and grow up. I can go for a while as if things are okay as long as I am controlling the food and ignoring what is really going on. But when I think about it I can just see this battle going on for ever. I feel so useless, so selfish. I want to punish myself but the only way I know ends up hurting others more than it does me so ends up more like a selfish reward - a way of switching off so that I can cope and don't give a damn about anything else. And it's been over a year now a year of tormenting my parents, playing for sympathy and failing at everything. I seriously would kill myself if it wasn't for Mum and Dad. I can't even love others like I am because I'm too self-preoccupied too scared. What can I do?

Things improved as time went by, as I built new friendships and relationships and found some sense of my self.

At the end of university, I wrote the following story. Perceptive readers may notice the tiniest hint of autobiography.

A story

What is life? A much pondered question yet the one that still manage to occupy the majority of Marianne's thoughts in her post-finals, post-graduation state, now that she was actually meant to be living it. Previously, decisions had been easy; getting A-levels, going to university had been expected, seen as the 'right' things to do. She had not particularly enjoyed university in the way that one is meant to. Her obsessive conscientiousness had led to too much work and too little play. As for the great idea of having time to 'find herself', she had spent most of the time looking forward to an era after university when that would be possible. Somehow, she had felt massively suffocated by academia and intellectualism. In comparison with those of her teachers and contemporaries, her ideas had seemed banal and inferior. Yet at the same time, there had always been a feeling that her academic career had been a shamefully solipsistic farce anyway, especially with regard to the study of literature; how could the most intelligent individuals in society devote themselves to pondering the intricacies of existence when they could have been trying to solve the more pressing problems in life such as poverty and injustice? Usually such challenging thoughts were held back from being expressed, however.

17

Marianne told herself that she obviously wasn't clever enough to see the real value of literature and study and should therefore just keep quiet on the subject. She emerged into postgraduate life full of contradictions; on the one hand she was determined to do something to improve society but on the other hand experiences in holiday jobs had told her that she'd never really be satisfied with the sort of job that would leave no time for contemplation. Rather hypocritically, at the same time as condemning the solipsism of existential thinkers who could devote themselves to abstract philosophical ideas, she knew that there was within her a need to constantly question her existence, motives and her desires. She knew from the books she'd been forced to read that her dilemma was nothing new; Goethe, Thomas Mann and Proust had all been tied in knots by the conflict between living life and thinking about it. She felt disappointed with them for failing to come up with entirely satisfactory answers. Goethe had indeed managed to be both artist and statesman but he had been by no means a socialist and seemed far more concerned with individual satisfaction than the common good, if she'd understood him correctly.

Another paradox in Marianne's thinking arose from a simultaneous desire to become famous and to sing and act her way to glory. How could she reconcile this with her need to be a social reformer? Could you argue that entertaining others was in its own way a means of making the world a 'happier' place and therefore socially acceptable? She was not entirely convinced. In fact, her reading of Brecht had enabled her to find another potential solution to the conflict; she would gain fame as an actress and then set up a theatre group for deprived children, attempting to improve her corner of the world and setting a good example to others through the power of theatre… But lack of confidence in herself made her dubious as to the likelihood of her ever achieving such goals. The world was full of better singers and actresses than her and even those that didn't have her voice were certainly superior in terms of looks and personality.

The third spanner in the works of Marianne's mind was the knowledge that deep inside she was motivated above all not by high-minded ambitions but by a desire to be loved. Surely if the right man would come along, she'd feel completely satisfied loving him, being loved and loving their children. But she secretly felt that no one would ever replace the love provided during childhood by her parents; no one would ever be able to love her strange looks, her strange ideas and her constant need for reassurance.....

As for having children, she only really ever contemplated this in her dreams, because she knew that in reality, any offspring to come from her would be as unbalanced as their mother...

Thus, Marianne's thoughts on life were muddled to say the least, and constituted primarily of a series of questions.

1. Is life about personal satisfaction or providing others with satisfaction?

2. Is life something you experience or think about?

3. Are we superior to animals in that we can be satisfied by cerebral achievements or is every woman at heart destined only to be happy as a mate and mother?

Time and food had to fit into the equation of Marianne's life at some point too. She had a good relationship with neither. The question of time was linked inextricably to that of death. She could not relax in the knowledge that death was almost certain to be years away but instead believed that her every action and plan had to be made to conditionally in the hope that she wouldn't be killed the next day. In fact, this terror of death extended to a horror of the death of those close to her and she felt that losing anyone in our family would induce in her a paralysis as numbing as any caused by her own fatality. Wasn't this natural in the modern world of wars, diseases and cataclysmic disasters?

The irony of all this was the fact that through her bad relationship with food, she had actually come closer to causing her own death than external factors I ever managed. An underlying feeling of 'fatness' during her late teens had blossomed into anorexia when she had left home. From 10 stone her weight had dropped to 6 and only threats of hospitalisation and force-feeding by her parents had got her back to some 'normality'. The obsession with body size and food had lasted throughout university and partly prevented the normal development which might have made Marianne a more 'rounded' person (an interesting turn of phrase).

By the end of her university career, she had allowed her weight to reach pre-anorexic levels and eating was no longer anywhere near as problematic as it had been. Yet she still felt very negative about her shape and very frustrated by her inability to give in to her insatiable appetite without gaining weight.

Wasn't she just a selfish middle-class princess who had it all but wanted more? Couldn't she see that her hang-ups were entirely self-induced and shameful in the face of real problems such as poverty, abuse and neglect?

Yes, in fact, she could, but somehow it didn't stop her feelings from occasionally taking over and preventing her from counting her blessings. So she was confronted with another age old dilemma of poets and artists; how do we silence our emotions and listen to our intellects when our feelings can't be trusted? And are our intellects really enough to make us into the people we'd like to be?

Freedom and loneliness were also contradictory factors in Marianne's life. On the one hand she loved the notion of being as free as a butterfly. Free to eat as she wanted: chocolate at 2 a.m. and raw carrots for breakfast; free to listen to Madonna one moment and Mozart the next. But being free also seemed to imply being alone and therefore unhappy. How would she ever maintain a relationship with anyone if she insisted on holding on to her idiosyncratic obsessions and rituals? The problem was that without them she didn't really believe that she would be able to cope. They were fail-safe methods that she had developed to stop her from allowing the things that worried her to control her life. To keep a check on her weight obsession, for example, she insisted on doing yoga exercises three times a day and would get distinctly tense if unable to do them. To deal with her death fears, she would spend the last few moments before sleep praying to some higher force for the safety of her family. (And this in spite of her total inability to believe in God). The freedom to do these things seemed vital to her, although she realised that few men would put up with such symptoms of potential madness. Would it be necessary to compromise? It seemed so.

But then again, finding a man in her postgraduate state of spinsterhood might present its own set of problems.

What was she doing wrong? Basically she knew that she was too unrelaxed to be able to sustain a relationship; too introspective and demanding. If only she could be different... yet in reality that seemed as much of a request as asking a zebra to be spotted.

19

Maybe she should simply use her theatrical skills to become a fun loving, uncomplicated girlfriend? But in all honestly, no life seemed preferable to such a life of masks.

Yes, she had contemplated suicide; mainly in her maddest, anorexic days, but also sometimes since, when it seemed as though life alone wasn't worth living. She had always rejected the idea eventually, pleading an inability to hurt her family as defence. To begin with, she had also expressed the conviction that there had to be some hope of things getting better, of her prince arriving, of reaching the land over the rainbow. Such hopes had gradually faded with the passing years, however, and now she only wished that the relative pessimism of her early twenties would not increase but level out. If not, she was not sure that she would be able to think of enough reasons to keep going any more.

Why such unbounding unhappiness in one so young? Objectively, she had it all; a good family, a good degree, the world at her feet... Yet subjectively she knew that she lacked those things that could make her really content (if real contentment was anything more than a myth, which she sometimes doubted).

Her ability to make friends was by no means adequate. She constantly doubted those friendships which by all normal standards were running smoothly, or she demanded far more from them than they deserved to give. More often than not, she heard indirectly that people actually liked her and felt amazed by the news. And even if she could force herself to accept such a discovery, it did not prevent her from plunging into crippling doubts at the onset of a new relationship. Not surprisingly then, she often annoyed or perplexed others with her paranoia.

(Perhaps a narrative comment would be appropriate here. Doesn't it seem, looking back over the last few pages of evidence, that Marianne's problem was above all an inability to like herself? Wasn't it just possible that her life would have been happier if it wasn't so conditional on the acceptance of others and more conditional on self-acceptance (which was, after-all, much more within her control?) But how would she achieve this switch from other-praise to self-praise? And might it not lead to a negative build-up of too much self-love in the long run? This was certainly Marianne's fear, whenever anyone suggested she should like herself more (this suggestion not being unique to the narrator but having been offered by various psychiatrists, counsellors and sympathetic friends over the years).

So as not to paint a too pessimistic picture of Marianne's existence, it has to be added that she did experience some days which would classify as 'happy'. Those are the days when she was with others who made her feel liked; often when she was involved in a play and surrounded by a communal spirit that came close to resembling that inherent in a good family life. Strangely, despite her lack of confidence in one-to-one relationships with men, she felt her happiest in groups of males. Thus, one of the 'up' times in her life had been when she'd been singing in a band with four of the opposite sex. Nothing particular had developed with any of them, but she had enjoyed the possibility of flirting as and when she wanted.

When she looked back on such formative experiences, she was shocked to realise how much more relaxed she had been about life and relationships back then. All of the men in the band had been fairly attractive and two of them had shown a desire to be more than just friends with her; it was only a feeling that they weren't quite 'Mr Right' that had stopped Marianne from doing anything.

Now by contrast, she felt that she could not afford to turn down any male advances, seeing as they were so few and far between.

Her first experience of love and heartbreak had come with of a brief, passionate encounter just before she had started university. It had been doomed from the start because he was someone else's boyfriend and, worse still, the boyfriend of a friend. This ruled out her allowing herself to be really in love at the time, although in retrospect she decided that she probably never could love anyone more again. Ironically, heartbreak arose when, rather than going back to his old girlfriend, he had found somebody new and ended up moving in with her, giving Marianne the excuse that the distance between the two of them was impractical and that he needed the security and convenience of being with somebody geographically closer.

One of Marianne's major concerns was how people got and stayed together in couples. One of her counsellors had suggested that in fact any one person could end up with any one of a number of partners, depending on circumstances like time and place. This disturbed Marianne somewhat, although she secretly felt that it was a more realistic view point than her own idealistic one which involved fate and the notion that everyone has a Mr or Mrs Right out there for her or him somewhere. She liked the notion expressed in Milan Kundera's 'Unbearable Lightness of Being' that we are all a half of one being and spend our lives looking for our 'other half'. But she nevertheless doubted the efficacy of this system and couldn't contemplate how people actually singled one another out. Above all, she doubted that anyone would ever choose her from amongst the realms of beautiful and secure people all around her.

One day at her lowest ebb Marianne made a decision. She had been treated badly by others in various situations. Realising that her dependency on others was once again making her unhappy and leaving her feeling lonely and rejected, she decided that the only solution now and for always would be to take control of her own destiny and work only on pleasing herself without the shaky support of others. Whilst this initially seemed like a selfish decision, she realised that it would not in fact preclude a kind of generosity towards others since she knew that ultimately she could only be happy by making others happy.

Her decision inspired her to sit down and write a list of the things which had to be changed according to new regime:

1. She would no longer be able to rely on the praise or acquiescence of others when choosing what to do.

2. She would no longer be able to use dieting and weight control as a substitute for controlling her life; after all they were methods based on standards of beauty decided by others and not by herself. To use them as regulatory methods was indeed a roundabout way of delegating self-control elsewhere.

3. She would have to decide that independent happiness was a possibility for her and that she could not wait for Mr Right before making a real go at life.

4. She would have to accept that life is both pain and happiness and that pure moments of either are far and few between. By most standards, in fact, her life was far over weighted on the side of happiness and she had blessings which it was perversity not to count.

To quote the words of a perceptive psychiatrist: life is like the tide; it goes up and down, in and out but always flows on.

Marianne's choice to alter her lifestyle did not bring instant results.

She spent a long period living in doubt and insecurity, feeling as though she'd never be able to like herself in the way she knew was necessary, if she were to be able to do anything really effective in life. But by gradually reassuring herself of her reasoning and forcing herself to think things through, time and again, she managed eventually to present a stronger and more confident image to the world that in turn enabled her to believe in that image.

She decided to go ahead and work towards a goal of setting up a children's theatre, on the condition that she would always be able to change direction later if it didn't prove as satisfying as she had hoped. She gave up on a search for a partner and decided to leave it to fate. Maybe he would arrive, maybe not....but there was no point in wasting time waiting. After all Marianne realised that time was her life. She remembered John Lennon's famous words about life and other plans. She decided that for her, this wasn't enough and she instead settled on her own definition of that elusive mystery which has puzzled great thinkers across history:

Life is me, now, making the best of what I have and what I can do and taking the contributions of others along the way, if and when they choose to make them.

Part Six

<u>My gap year between leaving school and starting university.</u>

Memories.

The summer of 1987. Watching a film about a girl dying of anorexia. Saying to my father that something like anorexia could never happen to me.

The rest of that summer a mad haze of friends, fun, love, hope of things to come. And then everything began to change.

Diary extracts

6th September 1987. Abroad

Despite the fact that the majority of the events that have taken place during the first 18 years of my life have gone unrecorded, I've decided that the next of months should not be forgotten. Whilst I cannot possibly tell what events will occur during my stay here, I intend to make the most of this great opportunity.

Well, I have now been here for two weeks minus the day and it's weird the way time seems to vary in length. Sometimes on good days is it definitely seems like I have only been here for a couple of days whilst at other times when I'm feeling homesick I feel like it's been months.

I must admit I really miss home. I realise now what good friends Mum and Dad are to me and it's hard not having them around. Obviously I miss my friends a lot too but Dad was right all those times that he said that he and Mum are my best friends in the world. There is not one day yet but I haven't cried at least once. I hope it's not going to be like this all year. Sometimes I just feel so lonely. It's weird how my feelings are up and down; sometimes I feel very positive and great but other times are awful. I know for sure that I've got a whole year ahead of me here so I suppose I'll just have to enjoy it. I just really feel like I need someone to get close to; I don't care if I don't have lots of friends I just want to meet someone I really like and can talk to.

13th September

Help what is happening to me.... another low day. I woke up yet again feeling really depressed but I cheered up when I phoned home; I actually managed to talk to Mum without crying which is good.

24th September

Today I got a phone call to say that I am finally into university! I'm so thrilled it's everything I wanted I've been on cloud nine ever since. I just really wish I was at home with Mum and Dad to celebrate.

4th October

Today was one of the saddest days of my life. I phoned home to discover that Grandad has died. Apparently after being in a coma for two weeks he died on Friday. I'm finding it so hard to bear because I'm such a long way away. When Mum told me I felt so upset that I can't be with them and Grandma. She must be so miserable; she loved him so much I can't cope with the fact that after going visiting them together for all these years I'm never going to see Grandad again. The funeral is going to be on Thursday. I feel awful that I won't be there. I hope Grandma will understand. I know that I could fly back if I really wanted to but if I did I don't think I'd ever be able to come back here afterwards. That said Grandma doesn't expect me to so I suppose I don't need to feel bad about it…. but I just feel guilty that I won't be there.

My boss has been very sweet and gave me a big hug and let me cry as much as I needed. She also give me sleeping pills to help me sleep and offered to let me take tomorrow off but I said no as I need something to keep me distracted. Tonight I feel so sad and homesick. I never realised before how horrible death is. Poor, poor Grandma; she is the one I feel most sorry for. I think Grandad would have been glad to get away from all the suffering. I loved him so much.

18th October

I've just come back from spending the weekend away with friends we had a great time the weather was gorgeous and the city is beautiful we saw loads and it was really lovely. I got on so well with the people I was with. We did a huge amount and by the end we were exhausted. We ate mostly junk food and I feel gross. My belly is huge but at least the food was cheap.

19th October

Today I began my diet and ate only good things, very low calorie I even resisted the apple crumble except for a small bowl-full and I made that the minimum fat and sugar. Let's hope I can keep it up.

20th October

Went out for ice cream with friends but I was very good I had a Diet Coke while they all had ice-creams. I still feel very fat though.

21st October.

Went out with a friend for lunch although I didn't eat anything. Still no effect though I still have a huge spare tyre. I weigh 140 pounds.

22nd October

Went out for lunch at but just had a Diet Coke.

Broccoli yoghurt and an apple for dinner.

23rd October

Went out to a bar with friends. We had a really good time dancing and getting drunk. Unfortunately I didn't meet anyone, although all the others seem to get chatted up by various men. I think the fact I'm too fat puts men off me. Before, the only good thing about me was slimness but now that's gone I've got nothing. I was actually quite good again today and I went without lunch although I had a bit of a binge in the evening (not on bad food though). I still need to persevere though it doesn't seem to have made any difference yet.

26th October

This evening I went to French class which wasn't too bad though I'm very tired. I'm still feeling as if I can't cope with the fact that I've got over 42 more weeks of this to go. Also I've had no post for days which is really getting to me. I'm still too fat but my diet is making a difference it seems.

25th December

Well I have no excuse for not having written for two months other than being lazy. A lot has happened in actual fact but to cut a long story short it has been a very difficult time. I suppose the fact that I'm not home for Christmas is making me feel especially sad and pensive but to be quite honest I do wonder how I'm going to get through another eight months of this. Today I'm feeling a real mixture of emotions because although I feel terribly homesick and I miss home so much that it hurts I also know that I'm very lucky to be doing what I'm doing and having the experience as I am aged 18.

The good news is that I've lost a lot of weight and hav got down to 120 pounds.

This holiday all I've eaten is vegetables but I can honestly say that I'm not hungry any more.

4th January

I'm down to 115 pounds. It must be the 700 cals a day. I know that I should really be eating more and I do feel a bit tired but I really don't want to put it back on. I don't know what to do; I don't know how much I can eat to maintain my weight. Why can't I just go back to being able to eat normally? Oh well at least I don't feel so overweight any more. I mean I don't feel thin but I don't feel so fat either.

10th February

Am 106 pounds but it seems to be stuck there even though I don't eat much. God knows what would happen if I even tried to eat the 1500 cals a day I could supposedly eat to maintain my weight. I am obsessed with food now it's really pissing me off.

11th February

I am feeling exhausted and very frustrated as I want to be upbeat and enthusiastic but I'm lethargic and have no patience. I really don't know what to do. I know I should be eating more and I honestly can't think about anything but food all the time but I can't bring myself to eat over 500 cal. My skin is really dry and I'm very tired but I just can't bear the thought of getting fat again - even now my bum and legs have flab on them. I was thinking about going to the doctor about it but it would really cost too much and besides I don't know what they'd say. I really want to talk to someone about it but it's so hard. Maybe it's really nothing to worry about and I should just put up with the tiredness for the sake of being thin. I just feel that food is running my life; every meal I dread because I feel so guilty about eating and having people watch me eat. It's horrible. The only advantage is that I haven't had a period in ages. Although I suppose in reality that isn't good either. I wish I'd never started dieting in the first place.

13th February

I felt tired and sick and I nearly didn't last the day. I didn't eat all day I just didn't feel like it which I guess is stupid but at least I don't feel guilty. I don't know which is worse - feeling fat or ill. To be honest, I feel like curling up and dying.

15th February.

I have talked to my boss about my worries about eating and she said that she is worried about me too and I'm definitely anorexic. She says that if I really don't feel I can force myself to eat, I will have to have therapy and if I don't get well she will have to send me home. She says it's a really serious problem and that she can't let it go on any further. I don't honestly think that it's serious as she makes out in that I haven't totally stopped eating and I'm not really skinny and yet I am worried and I don't feel I can solve the problem alone. I feel dreadful I don't want to cause hassle and yet I know it's becoming an obsession which I can't stop.

8th April 1988

It is now 7.10 a.m. English time and I'm on the plane. Thank god only an hour to go. It's been an awful journey and I have felt very uncomfortable with really bad pain in my shoulder and leg and no chance to move around. I'm in a window seat with two sleeping men to my right and no chance to even go to the toilet. I'm feeling pretty tired. I hope I won't be too tired when I eventually get home but I just couldn't sleep. I couldn't eat the plane food but I ate some apples and yoghurts. So all in all I got to a thousand and seventy five calories yesterday which makes me feel terrible and yet I know that I have to keep eating now that I've got this far. I feel so apprehensive about actually going back. My feelings are so up and down, making me feel excited and optimistic to tearful and depressed from one minute to the next. I know that going back home isn't going to make everything okay miraculously but I know that having come home I now really owe it to everyone to get better so I'm really going to try. I just hope Mum and Dad will understand and not expect too much too soon. Still I'm sure I can get medical help on the National Health Service so if it needs it I can always go away for a while. Not that I really feel ill in myself but I just don't want to cause them hassle or let them down after all this. I just hope they won't make me fat all at once though. The worst thing I'm feeling at the moment is real anxiety attacks they seem to come and go all of a sudden and make me feel totally panicky and scared. Oh well not long now. Help me.

The other thing I hope is that they won't be too shocked when they see me. I honestly don't think I look that different but other people say differently. Still, I'm still physically healthy so that's the main thing. My only slight worry is that my hair really seems to have suffered and appears to be falling out at rather an alarming rate when I brush it or pull it. Maybe it's just the after-effects of 7 1/2 months of having a perm though. It just needs a good cut.

9th April

Now been home for just over a day and I'm feeling such a terrible amount of contradictions. Getting off the coach was so emotional - just to see and hug Mum and Dad was the best feeling and yet it was tied up with the immeasurable guilt of having given in and come home. Although they were noticeably shocked at my appearance, I'm sure the jetlag had a lot to do with making me seem tired because really I'm not that thin. Anyway the last two days have been spent talking and talking and I've been honest with them about everything and I've agreed that I must totally trust them for a few weeks in order to start the process of recovery. The only problem is that still deep inside I don't feel thin or want to put on weight even though I know that it's part of the cure and I do want to be free of this. I just feel I really don't deserve to eat or get well after all I've put everyone through. Mum has been giving me completely normal meals which has been awful; I can't breathe when I eat and I can't bear to chew the food because tasting it is indulging myself which I just don't deserve. I weigh 6 stone 9 at the moment but I'm sure it's bound to rocket with all the food I am eating as Mum really doesn't realise how many calories she is making me eat. I feel such a terrible contradiction – when I am with them and talking I know that they are the rational ones, it's just so hard when I am by myself. I love them so much and I feel so guilty for what I am putting myself through. It makes me hate myself even more. I just can't help myself from panicking when I get by myself.

It is so ironic I want to be well and free of this so that I won't be such a burden to them and yet I really don't deserve to be happy - no one else really ever is anyway and I'm just deceiving everyone into thinking I have a problem.

16th April

I hate the thought of having to spend a whole weekend with my parents and yet I hate myself for thinking that too because I know that they are so lovely and are trying to help me. I just don't deserve it.

1. I'm selfish I only ever think of me.

2 I'm deceitful I have always deceived people into thinking I'm wonderful and now I'm deceiving them into thinking I'm ill.

3. I'm not worthy of such kind caring parents.

4. I've given in to my selfish desires and now if I get fat it's all my own doing.

5. I'm not ill. Just a bit underweight and selfish.

17th April

Last night they tried to make me eat loads because I hadn't managed to put on the weight and it just made me feel so tense. I ended up throwing my pudding across the room and breaking down – which was so weak and selfish of me. I upset them so much and yet they are trying too hard to help me. I feel so confused – for the first time this morning I felt tired and fed up with it and let myself lie in bed – but now I feel ashamed of doing that and being lazy.

I see no real solution to my problem because there are always two voices inside my head - one which tells me that I should want to put on weight and rest and be nice to mum and dad and give in to my weakness and another which reminds me that I'm selfish and not really ill and not worthy of all the time I'm getting. At the same time there is also the fact that no matter how hard I try I don't feel thin and I can't bear the thought of eating without knowing the calories or putting on weight. I think maybe I'm just spending too much time thinking about it all – again totally selfish.

How do I break the cycle?

23rd April

I woke up feeling tired and confused. All I want is to be a nice person and of use to others but the hard part is that I feel that deep down the real nature of me is horrible so it will never really be possible. I can be superficial with people most of the time and deceive them but those people that get to know me really well know that really I am impatient and nasty.

27th April

Dinner was tense all I could think was fat fat fat and how my jeans felt tighter. Mum got me to sit down in the living room afterwards but we didn't even talk. She realises what a waste of time it is. She keeps going on about me being ill. It's a joke because I'm not. I know I'm fine I'm just deceiving everyone. I'm going to bed now I'm not really tired but I can't bear any more of today. I'm totally getting into laziness and selfishness. I hate myself.

28th April

I woke up at five then dozed till 6:30. I feel fine today. I went shopping and got my hair cut. It looks very boring but I don't care. This afternoon I'm going to cut the lawn. I don't need to relax as I'm not tired. I just feel guilty and indulgent after yesterday. I wish I could weigh myself. I'm sure I'm 7 1/2 stone now. I feel so fat.

29th April

Mum talked to me today. She told me off for keeping busy all day doing cleaning and gardening and not allowing myself to relax. She said that my mind is exhausted and confused and needs peace and quiet to sort out rationality from irrationality. Each time I don't relax I am avoiding doing the one thing that would really make me well. She said that this is taking the easy way out. I just feel so scared. Deep inside I want to do nothing and relax but then I feel guilty.

I'm so scared of life and of getting fat and of giving in.

Mum says the root of my illness lies in not wanting or trying to be happy and working hard on useless jobs to avoid thinking about getting better and being happier. But why should I want to be happy in a world where no one really ever it is and where it's all so scary? I just want to hide away- but then I'm sure everyone does but no one gives in just because life has to go on and we have to be strong.

I just feel so useless.

29th April

Glimmer of hope. This evening mum and dad forced me to go out and see a musical at the Art Centre and for a while things seemed a lot more hopeful. I really enjoyed it and the singing and dancing reminded me of the things are used to love doing. It was really good. Mum also sat me down and told me to buck up my ideas and try harder to eat more as my weight was only seven stone with clothes this evening. I had another binge to please her- two mars bars, a bounty, an ice cream and a big glass of milk and orange juice. I now feel disgusting and a bit depressed again but at least it's bedtime.

30th April

5.30a.m. I woke up really early this morning feeling depressed and confused again but then I thought of the show last night and it stopped things from seeming quite so bad. There ARE good things in the world.

I do want to keep thinking positive about nice things. As the psychiatrist said, only by feeling nice in myself can I be nice to others. It is hard when the black thoughts keep coming back and everything seems so scary and I don't feel ill. Still, here are some aims for today:

1. To be patient and nice and not horrible to Mum and Dad.

2. To try to forget my body.

3. To try and remember the amazing music and dancing from yesterday and also remember the way that I used to be able to sing to entertain people and get such a thrill from it.

4th May

Thoughts:

People may never really be happy but it is better to be unhappy and still be able to function in life without crazy obsessions and being a worry to others than to be unhappy and wallow in self-pity and shirk responsibility. If you don't try and be happy you can't hope to be, I suppose, and at least by being useful and active, you can try to help make others happy.

My goal now is to try and find a balance. Not to be too thin, not to be too fat. Not to reject food totally but not to over eat. Not to try and do everything but not to give up everything by cutting myself off. Not to love or like everyone but not to love or like no one. To love those who are really important.

Not to allow myself to be affected by lots of unimportant people but not to ignore those who really care. Not to think life is all happiness but not to think life is all unhappiness. Not to think of myself too much but not to totally reject my true feelings and desires. Not to take on too much responsibility but not to reject responsibility. Not to worry too much about the future but try to plan it so it will be as successful as possible

Not to dwell on the past mistakes but to learn by experience.

And yet, despite writing so rationally, why am I still scared of putting on weight and eating?

I just wish I knew who I am and who I ought to be and what I want.

5th May

Feel disgusting. Went out to tea with an ex teacher and she gave me 3 cakes to eat. Feel guilty and disgusting.

7th June

Frustrating day. I felt lonely but persisted in planning my day to include yoga, reading and a visit to the hairdressers. I found myself longing the hours away and feeling indulgent and fat but I had to resist selfish feelings even though I still felt uncomfortable. I also went for a short run today which felt something of an achievement. I must admit that things have seemed brighter and clearer the last few days although I still lack energy and have a sinking feeling very often. I now yearn to get out and be a bit more part of life again although, it does still scare me rather especially as regards to socialising and eating. But I know I have to work at it soon in order to be ready for university.

Having been anorexic for five months and having caused immense upset amongst those who love me and having achieved nothing, it seems time to decide to have a concerted fight to give it up. It's so easy to pretend to want to be free of it and to go through the motions of eating and putting on weight. Having gained 1 1/2 stone I now look relatively normal. And yet I know damn well that unless I face it now I will allow myself to sink down again the minute I leave home because until now I haven't really thought it through and done the things which will enable me to get better. Mum and Dad have tried so hard and been so encouraging and yet they now can't give any more and my selfishness can't be allowed to upset the family any further. I don't know why I haven't been able to make myself try harder up until now. Maybe it's because of pig-headedness or maybe I simply wasn't ready. I spent weeks and weeks lying because I couldn't find the courage to say "screw it all" and force myself to do the things which will turn me into a person again. Because that's what anorexia does. It stops you being a person. Sure, I have gone through the motions of life, pushing myself to extremes. I have spent useless hours cleaning, revising for hours upon end, running until I ache and yet none of those things make me a real person. God knows what pushed me to become like that. I don't think it was all down to my experiences abroad although turning myself into an automaton there was very useful because it enabled me to ignore my real feelings when I was so homesick. But I think things began to go wrong at the end of the Lower Sixth when I went on a summer music course and I suddenly seem to have lost my confidence and bounce. Of course things weren't so extreme then but from then on I began to hide in my room wasting time on work and cutting myself off.

Of course, it got results in a material sense and good exam results all round. And yet by that time they didn't even seem good to me because I had stopped really thinking about things and channelled everything into becoming some kind of perfectionist. I wanted to go to university for all the wrong reasons - not because it would be a fun place to go but because it would make me look good and contribute well to this screwed up confused image of the person I wanted to be.

And then the body thing came along. Until my year abroad I had had little time to think about the physical side of me because I had concentrated on cultivating the intellect. I'd never been satisfied - I'd always felt fat and wanted to look like a model on the cover of a magazine. So when I had time to think about it I began to try to take that side of things in control. I got thinner but I suppose that when things didn't miraculously improve and I didn't look like a model just because I lost some weight, I pushed it further and further. Gradually the anorexia took over and the starvation spiral let me down and down. Now I'm no longer at a critical weight and haven't been for some time, it is hard to understand why eating seems so repulsive still. Yet I suppose I have to admit that it is a form of security. Eating is fun and fun is indulgence and perfectionists don't indulge themselves. The trouble is that no one is perfect. Everyone is just what they are and beyond a certain limit they can't improve themselves. It is like being a flower. You can nurture a flower and feed it and give it sun and it will be beautiful and if you neglect it, it will shrivel up. But you can never make it more than a flower. Everyone has limits and I have to face up to mine in order to achieve my full potential and live as a person.

Certainly, I have not even got halfway to my full potential by being anorexic. I've been unloving, cold, frightened and like a five year old instead of a nineteen year old. No one could call it proper living. I have always gone through life thinking 'I should be this' and 'I should do that' and feeling jealous without being thankful for what I am and could be. And in the last few months I haven't even asked what I want to be. Deep inside I want to be loving, caring and help others – a happy person who can be a friend to other people and participate in life to the full.

The trouble is that my 'perfectionist' side keeps pushing me to build a cool, controlled image because it tells me that successful people are like that. But when I think about it I know that those people in society and from history who I really admire and want to be like are not cold fishes: Ghandi was a deeply emotional spiritual person. Mozart was emotionally like a rollercoaster and even Mrs Thatcher, whose politics I hate but who deserves respect, cries in public and says what she feels even if she makes a fool of herself.

On the other hand those plastic people on the front of women's magazines who I sometimes feel jealous of in my irrational moments are rarely worthy of that jealousy.

So I cannot allow myself to go on punishing myself and others because of some insane jealousy. God knows I have so much more than many people and should use it in full. By staying anorexic I will stay cold and useless and dependent on others all my life. Of course things will go up and down but turning to anorexia isn't the answer when things go down. It feels scary to face up to it and make myself stop at all but if I don't I won't survive university or life.

I am what I am. I will never be an exceptional beauty so it is better to be healthy and make the most of what I have. I will never be an exceptional intellect so it's better to achieve as much as I can. I have to set my own realistic standards and not compare myself to others constantly. I can either decide to go to university to get a first and work every hour of the day and not complain because I'm having no fun or I can go with the idea of making the most of it intellectually and emotionally. Of course, I don't want to be lazy but there has to be a balance. Of course, I don't want to get fat but I can't let the scales rule my life, if over-eating occasionally means making me more acceptable and human to others. I have to take responsibility for myself in order to be human again.

It is something of a miracle that I was in any fit state to start university the following autumn. But start I did. With a set of rules.

Written by wonderful Mum and Dad, Autumn 1988:

Rules for survival at University.

1. *Read through these rules at least once a day. Think about them and abide by them. If you feel under pressure at any time, make yourself read through these rules.*
2. *Spend a period of at least 15 minutes each day relaxing. This means lying or sitting doing nothing but concentrating on yourself. If it helps, do relaxation exercises or listen to music. If this makes you cry don't worry.*
3. *Don't compare yourself to others. For you that activity is destructive as you only concentrate on certain aspects of other people but not the whole person. You are you with all your talents and abilities and you will never be anyone else.*
4. *Try to be honest with people. You will soon make friends. Find those in whom you can confide and then be as honest as you can. Tell them what you really feel rather than what you think you ought to feel. Learn to say no and yes.*
5. *Don't worry if you're not at the centre of things. Find those activities that you're really good at and enjoy such singing and concentrate on those. Try out new activities like sport but don't use exercise as a way of slimming or it becomes excessive. Have some fun every day.*
6. *Learn work patterns which enable you to survive. It is better to leave university with a third than a nervous breakdown. No one bothers about the class of degree once you've got it. Set an absolute maximum work time each day (not more than five hours) and stick to it rigidly. Try to work in short concentrated bursts with breaks between. Have a coffee, visit a friend. Set yourself time targets rather than 'objective' targets. For example work for an hour rather than finish a chapter. This is essential for you.*
7. *Remember that nobody at university does all the work set. It is not expected of you and it is impossible. Work out priorities.*
8. *If you feel under pressure, firstly try to relax. Start by breathing etc. If this doesn't work, seek help. Talk to a friend, a tutor, or phone home. Remember that the high standards which you set are only determined by you.*
9. *You have done nothing in your life about which you need to feel guilty apart from having anorexia. You have had no harmful lasting effects on anyone, so there is no need to feel guilt.*
10. *You must have rigid rules about eating which you stick to totally. You must eat three full meals a day and snacks. Don't count calories but have a maximum and minimum weight band. For example 8 stone 4 to 8 stone six. You must decide on this before you go and adhere to it strictly. Counting calories is a form of mental illness.*
11. *If you follow the rules you will have total control over your life and survive university.*
12. *Remember that whilst all those around you are bright, so are you. They too will have their problems and they will also be thinking that everyone around them is brighter including you.*

Part Seven

<u>Childhood</u>

Memories

Happy times with a loving, protective and nurturing family who supported me in everything I did. A life full of music, books, travels, house exchanges, cats, running, eating and living well and normal childhood concerns and follies.

A memory, aged 12. Kissing a French boy by a large oak tree.

And then every night feeling dirty, guilty. Praying to a god in whom I did not believe to forgive me and make me feel clean again. Night after night after night.

And memories of each night ending with an anxious ritual throughout my childhood. A prayer to a God that I did not believe in to protect and keep each member of my family safe. Each one named individually... But then an overwhelming superstitious fear on falling asleep that someone had been forgotten and would suffer because I had not done my bit to protect them......

And a sense of guilt. A deep rooted, free floating sense of having been bad.

Diary entries

7ᵗʰ January 1983

Aged 13

I'm gonna have to stop eating bounties etc otherwise I'll put on even more weight. It's the trials for the school play on Tuesday I would love to get a part I'd like a big one but I know I won't get one.

10ᵗʰ January

School again. A rather average day. S wants to go out with a 21-year-old! I reckon she's a blinking idiot. P is trying to talk her into it but to be honest I reckon boys aren't worth worrying about.

13ᵗʰ January

So far this diary has been heck of a boring; sorry I'm an average person! I had a swearing fit today (under my breath) and I hate it it's really disgusting. When I think about it I feel really rather low. Late New Year's resolution: stop swearing or be classed horrible!!!!

16ᵗʰ January

Today I got my second period. I had to go out during church as I felt ill. I spent quite a lot of the day doing homework. Oh dear I can't really think of anything else to write.

20th January

I am beginning to hate myself. No one seems to like me anymore; friends or teachers especially Mrs V, Mr W, Mr X, Mr Y and Mrs Z. Dad says it's paranoia or something. I know what it is really. Me!

11th July

Dress rehearsal. Went ok. I got a big part in the end: really chuffed. I have made 2 really good friends doing the play.

19th July from music camp

The food here is great! Just thought I'd mention it. I have discovered another nice boy called N. He is really sweet. I have also made loads of new friends. It is really fantastic. We went swimming a lot today.

16th August - Holiday in France

A whole day doing 'rien' except for a little shopping. We did however break up the laziness by going for a meal out. It was delicious and so was the waiter but I think he was a little too old 'pour moi'. Shame though....

29th August

At the moment my life seems to be taken up with talking French, falling out with my pen friend and arguing with Mum and Dad.

Memories

A memory of being 13 and at secondary school. A sudden decision to be just like an older friend. To excel at music, drama and academia. To get to a prestigious university. To become head girl. To push myself.

The normal teenage insecurities of a 15 year old girl – loves, friendships, insecurities, highs and lows.

Diary entries

1985 Aged 15

1st January

Another year gone. Saw in the New Year with friends. Had amazing time. Left party at 2.45 a.m. and went for a sleepover! C was lovely to me. D swore undying love to me. Nevertheless my affections are all pointed at E. Have to learn how much I can trust him though.

4th Jan

Painted my room. L rang and we went to town. Bought a slaggy grey skirt. God knows why. Did biology essays. Watched tv. Ate curry. Went to bed.

5th Jan

I am beginning to think there is something wrong with me. 1. My hair is always a mess. 2. I'm getting uglier. 3. I'm getting fatter. 4. My clothes are all horrible. 5. All my friends are going off me.

Bloody, bloody piss boring horrible life. I hope it starts to get better soon.

13th January

Am very happy. Feel really good. I'm in love. I'm also doing homework and it is going really well.

21st January

I passed my O-level maths with a B!!!!!!!!!!!!!!!!!!!!!!!

X came into my lesson and kissed me! 69% in my music exam. Life is going up, up, up! Wow! Late New Year's resolution: I will cheer up.

23rd Feb

Absolutely exhausted. Worked all day then went to town and bought a file. Wow. I HATE WORK.

24th Feb

Homework all day. Choir in the evening. Pretty ok.

25th Feb

School. X ignored me. Come to think of it everyone ignored me except R. Oh dear. I think my personality has changed for the worst.

13th April

(On a trip abroad with Mum)

Lovely day in the sun, visiting museum, a lake and a fab Italian restaurant. Sad to be leaving.

4th May

Dyed my hair. Bloody hell. It came out a kind of pink/orange colour. Mum and dad didn't quite know what to say. Oh dear.

Sunday boring Sunday. Homework and revision.

5th May

Monday boring Monday. Homework and revision. Couldn't sleep.

16th May

Another incredibly boring day. I think I'm going to have to stop writing every night. I haven't got time every night with all the work. Sorry dearest diary.

24th July

Long time no hear! Well, a lot has happened since those dreaded O-levels. I don't think I've done half as well in them as I could've done. Still there's always retakes. Now I just have to wait for the results. August 22 I do believe.

At the moment I am utterly exhausted. I'm working Monday and Friday mornings in the bakery and evenings in the pub serving food and washing up. I'm getting slowly fatter and weigh eight stone two or three. I'm going on holiday for two weeks on Saturday with the family. I'm looking forward to it a little. I am still unloved and unwanted and therefore depressed but never mind, I can handle it.

Memories

A memory of a family summer holiday, aged 16. A spell of insomnia. Long nights spent worrying, feeling scared, feeling deep-seated, free-floating guilt.

A memory of a summer in sixth form spent working abroad. A sudden wave of homesickness, depression and anxiety. Parents visiting and realising; taking me home and rebuilding me.

Diary entry.

August 1986

Well here I am halfway through my second week here. I honestly don't know how I'm going to survive the next two weeks, The children are okay but they are so impersonal. I really don't know why I am here. Today is my birthday. I think it's just about the worst ever. It was super to open Mum and Dad's presents but the kids didn't even wish me happy birthday. I really want to go home but the thing is that I keep thinking if I don't carry this through, I will never survive university. I don't know what's wrong with me really I ought to be able to just read and enjoy the peace but it's awful I just can't stop crying. I feel useless and in the way.

The beginning. The end.

A memory. Aged 7. A stranger but one who had been entrusted. A violation. A child's trust betrayed. In a matter of days, everything altered. A secret held and never to be told. The beginning and the end.

A year of living

It is now a year on from writing the first version of my Story. In the meantime, I have continued to write in a blog, cataloguing the ups and downs of living. Once again, I am reproducing what I wrote at the time unedited, except for typos; the lived experience of a woman forty years on from an experience that changed everything. Some would label me a woman 'in recovery' and in some ways I am; trying to recover the child I was before my innocence was taken away. Others would use the ACE acronym and define my forty years of struggle as a response to an Adverse Childhood Experience, which I also identify with. But if I had to define myself, I would choose to label myself as a woman in discovery. It is through writing and connecting with others over the past year that I have learnt more about myself than ever before.

It has not been the best of years: the heart-breaking deaths of young people with whom I worked through suicide; family illness; an increasing sense that I am in the wrong job and occasions where I have felt completely at odds with and disliked by colleagues; a feeling of homesickness and disconnection living so far from family and friends.

But many good things too; a beautiful family wedding; success in achieving a major professional development award with flying colours; a promotion to a job where I have the ability to make a real difference to the education of children and young people.

So here, a year of living in discovery.

About me and this blog

I am a mother, educator, manager, facilitator and creative artist living in the North. I write professional blogs with a particular focus on wellbeing, mental health and creativity. I have created this blog to accompany my recently self-published e-book 'The Story of My Self' which tells of my almost 40 year long struggle to overcome the effects of trauma, anxiety, depression and addictions. In this blog, I will provide weekly updates as to my progress. The blog is for me but also for you, if you have struggled or continue to struggle and want re-assurance that there is life beyond.

Posted on August 20, 2016

So here I am.

Having published my ebook and made the promises, I have decided that I am going to blog on a weekly basis with evidence of what I am doing to ensure that 'this time is different', that I don't slip back into bad habits and that the patterns that have become engrained over the last nearly forty years don't continue.

So, at the end of week one:

• Each morning I have started the day with a glass of water, a look out of the window at a big, solid tree and a thought of my book and why I must not forget it.

• I have delivered a staff training on child protection and I talked about the need, highlighted by numerous children's charities including the NSPCC, for adults to find ways to enable children to communicate when they have been abused. We need to take seriously the fact that, whilst abuse is bad, it is less bad for a child if they are not left to dwell on it for years. Bad things happen but we can move on from them if we are given support. I did not say it in the training, but I am living proof of what happens when bad things and trauma are hidden away and allowed to fester over years.

- I have not exercised manically every day. One day I came home and told the obsessive voices in my head ('you need to get out for your walk!!!!') to be quiet and bugger off while I drank a beer with my husband. Another day I took a slow, shuffling walk with my daughter as she needed a chat. The usual, strict, 30-minute power walk had to be abandoned and I had to tell the shouty voices to be quiet so that I could listen to her.

- I ate a scone in my morning break in front of people one day. The voices were there ('you are sooooooo indulgent, what will people think?') but I ignored them.

- Still at work at 6pm one night, I stopped and went home because I had done my agreed hours. The voices were there ('You haven't finished!! You'll regret it tomorrow!!'). But I stopped. Tomorrow was fine.

- One day I walked out of work on the dot of five to take my children to an appointment. The voices were shouting, again ('What will people think of you! If you don't work overtime and be the last to leave they'll think you are lazy!!') but I ignored them, held my head high and walked.

One foot in front of the other, day by day.

Posted on August 28, 2016

Weekly update.

Tuesday morning thoughts.

I have left my lunch at home. I usually bring a plain bagel and fruit.

I am worried about several work issues.

I could have stopped at a shop and bought a sandwich after I realised I had forgotten it.

I did not because I did not want to be judged by others for being 5 mins later into work than usual.

I could buy a sandwich in the canteen. I am worried that I will be judged if I do.

Wait. What? What?!!!!

5 minutes late??

Who will even notice?

For younger teachers to whom I set a role model, setting an 'example' of robotic rigidity is unhealthy.

I am not a robot.

Buying lunch. What does it matter if they judge me? They are not friends - I do not even know most by name.

And what might they think? She is greedy?

Why?

And actually, to buy and eat food they make is supportive, flattering, grateful.

Challenge it. Buy lunch.

————————————

And I did. I managed to work through my lunch break but as I was flying past the canteen to a post-lunch meeting I turned back. I went and bought a tuna sandwich. And I took 5 minutes to eat it. One of the canteen staff gave me a smile and said 'well done'. I remembered having told her last week that I have vowed to eat lunch every day; she had commented on the fact that I always seem to be on the go and need to take care to eat and keep up my energy levels.

She didn't say 'how greedy! A tuna sandwich!'.

She didn't judge me.

She said 'well done'.

And I say to myself 'well done'.

Posted on September 3, 2016

Packed lunches.

Each morning I get up and make my son a packed lunch. A carefully prepared wrap, chopped cucumber and tomato, olives and yoghurt. Sometimes a few crisps as a treat.

He has a cool bag with three zippy sections and fun little snap-top pots, each of which fits neatly and satisfying into the right section.

Each morning I throw a plain bagel into some cling film and shove it in my handbag, maybe with an apple, maybe not.

Why do I care for him so lovingly and not myself?

Because it is a habit. A bad habit.

So today there are two packed lunches with carefully made wraps.

I don't have the cool bag yet, but I am going to get one. With flowers on.

Posted on September 16, 2016

Hunger.

This week I have realised that I am hungry. Almost all the time. It is not something that I generally admit to because I have spent so long denying and ignoring it. But I have an almost raging hunger when I stop and take breath in the middle of a busy day.

I have developed a habit of biting the insides of my lips and I think that this is a substitute for eating.

So I am going to start to eat more.

I have continued with my fruit and wrap each day but I need more.

My tendency is to eat a lot at the end of the day but I am going to plan for more healthy, filling food earlier in the day.

I am hungry. For food. For life. For continuing to live life to the full.

Posted on September 23, 2016

Vulnerable.

It has been a long, hard week.

I frequently find that there is a mismatch between the world as I think it should be and the world as it is. I think that lots of us do: Twitter is full of likeminded individuals who share and support each other in the virtual world but reveal that the 'real world' does not accept them so willingly.

This week at work had been a case in point: I have tried to convince colleagues of the value of a different style of working with one another and our clients but have been challenged.

I know that change takes time to embed and that this is just the start of a long journey.

But it has been hurtful. I have talked of love, made myself vulnerable and asked challenging questions.

At times I have cried, wanted to hide and wanted to punish myself.

But I have managed to stay strong. Because I know that deep down, my values are sound and that I am being authentic. That I have a back story of shame, now written and shared, that I have owned and acknowledged. And that no-one can really shame or hurt you again once you have named and examined the things that have hurt you most deeply in the past.

So this week I have not reverted to the old patterns. I have eaten, allowed myself to rest and to experience uncomfortable feelings without them damaging me.

The nature of vulnerability means that we have to be both immeasurably weak and strong.

But it is the only way.

Posted on October 2, 2016

Feeling low.

I am feeling low this week. I am exhausted: work has been busy but my mind has also been working overtime. Worrying, overthinking and being overly negative and critical.

I am trying to carry on at work as if all is well but the strain is taking its toll at home. I am irritable with my children and husband. I am tearful and tired.

These are all warning signs that I need to allow myself to rest and stop.

My usual tendency is to throw myself into more work and punish myself.

But I will not.

I will go to bed early.

I will cut corners.

I will say no.

I will eat well and exercise less. A walk on Monday and Tuesday and a cycle on Thursday and Saturday.

I will force myself to slow down, notice and engage with everyday tasks.

I will force myself to give hugs, smiles and kind words to those in my family.

I will listen to music.

I will give thanks.

Today I found a folder full of projects I did in a previous job. Much as I feel useless and incompetent, I am not. I am still the person I was and more.

I will keep reading this.

I will also keep dipping into 'Reasons to Stay Alive' by Matt Haig and 'Positively Primal' by Emma Woolf.

And into my own Story.

And I will update next week.

Posted on October 10, 2016

You can mend too.

So the last week was phenomenally hard at work but, as Rudyard Kipling advocates, I pretty much managed to keep my head.

I stuck with last week's vow to be kind to myself and although others were not so kind to me, I held strong.

I had to deal with issues at work at relating to children who have suffered trauma and distress and although it was hard, I took courage from the fact that I understand the issues.

I ate well and resisted the temptation to push myself to exercise manically even though I was exhausted.

On this, World Mental Health Day, I have remembered that I am not alone and that it is crucial to keep mental wellness on the agenda. Having mental health difficulties does not make us weak or incapable: it makes us human and more resilient, as long as we recognise our difficulties and own them.

If someone is physically hurt, the bruising and pain can be minimised by the quick application of an ice pack. If someone has a stroke and quick action is taken, the effects can be dramatically limited and chances of full recovery can be hugely increased.

If we are hurt emotionally, long term psychological damage can be avoided if the pain is acknowledged and dealt with rather than ignored and repressed.

We need to make sure that someone is listening to and watching children closely so that they can share their secrets and pain before they develop into long term mental suffering.

I kept hold of my pain for too long and my wound got infected and festered. But now it is mended.

You can mend too.

Tell your story and learn from it.

Posted on October 15, 2016

Slaying the exercise demon.

As I type this from my exercise bike on a Saturday morning when I feel exhausted, both physically and mentally, I admit that I need to do something about this.

I can't take time off exercising.

I can play it down, make excuses, pretend it is 'healthy'; after all, I am only doing short spells of walking or cycling, I am not running excessively, my weight is healthy, I eat well. Etc etc etc.

But here's the thing. The thought of not exercising for more than a day still sends me into a tail spin.

The free- floating anxiety and negative voices use words like 'fat' and 'indulgent' but it is also a physical sensation. A physical feeling of nausea, panic. Tearfulness. Anger.

So this week I promise to tackle it.

I have a week off work. I am not ready to do a whole week without it but I am going to vow to walk on only two days: Sunday and Friday.

On Monday, Tuesday, Wednesday and Thursday I will do no planned exercise.

I will eat what I want.

I feel hugely anxious even writing this.

But it is long overdue.

See you on the other side.

Posted on October 18, 2016

Progress update.

Sunday

I got up this morning feeling tired, achey. I did my yoga and stretching and went for a walk. My knees and back ached.

Back home, I feel unsettled and jittery. I feel light headed, exhausted. Slightly depressed and irritable with waves of anxiety that are almost physical.

It is interesting to note that this is even after exercising.

I ate a big meal and had wine last night and my tummy is unsettled.

Monday

I went for another walk this morning and know that that was it until Saturday. I feel strangely exhilarated.

I am less tired today than I was yesterday.

I have also been reading about mindfulness and was particularly interested in this idea:

.....And what the research is showing that when we're not actually engaged in present with what we're doing, our minds just very naturally click off into this default mode, and that's that mind wandering, mental chatter, the judgement , the self-criticism, that kind of thing that we just find ourselves in throughout the day.....

I think that I certainly allow the 'mental chatter' to control me rather than me controlling it. The voices that tell me I am bad if I don't exercise, if I eat.

Tuesday

Woke up in a bit of a panic but did some mindfulness breathing and focused on the feelings in my body. Some waves of anxiety but brought my mind back to breathing. Son joined me for a hug in bed which would not have happened if I'd been out exercising.

Kept breathing and when I got up I did my stretches and continued with deep and mindful breathing.

Wandered to the shore with husband and dogs. Told him about my exercise 'cold turkey' and he pointed out that it is much nicer to have me stroll with him instead of ignore him and power off ahead of him on a 'walk' as I have done the last 2 days.

Of course my usual recourse to counteract missed exercise would be to miss out on food. A knee-jerk, instinctive, subliminally-programmed response. But I told myself that I deserve to eat, to be and put butter on my bagel.

And I am ok.

Lunch. A pasty. Disappointingly dry but eaten mindfully. Momentary moments of discomfort, panic, the voices. But reminding myself that these voices are not my voice. They do not control me.

Afternoon. Feeling under a bit of pressure as have visitors. Realise that that in itself is making me quite anxious and that my default setting would be to escape on a run/walk.

Perhaps my need to exercise is as much to with head space and needing to escape people as anything else.

Although I am endlessly fascinated by people and relationships, the reality of people (even loved ones, friends and family) is sometimes just too much.

What is that about? I think that much is to do with the fact that after years of cutting myself off from allowing myself to feel and live life in its fullness, I still find it hard to let myself relax, open up and risk showing myself to be happy without the associated critical, judgemental voices in my head.

And I guess that I also fear, as so often when people try to make changes in their lives, that others may judge/comment/criticise if I break the patterns that I have been stuck in for years.

But really? Does that really matter?

What might they say?

'You seem happier/less anxious/healthier/less obsessive?'

For the people who love me to see me happier: would that be such a bad thing?

For me to be happier: would that be such a bad thing?

Who is in charge here?

I need to keep going.

It's hard just now but I need to keep going….

Wednesday.

I have woken early. Thoughts and worries raging.

A wine-fuelled dinner last night and half arguments/half discussions about the state of the world/the state of education/ whether we can genuinely make a difference. The outcome a feeling of powerlessness, a voice out of sync with others, even those closest to me.

A half-written idea for a blog, anxious fears about training to be delivered next week.

Free floating panic.

And the usual answer would be to get up, in a sweaty haze and get out and walking or cycling….

But not today, because I have chosen not to.

The result is a feeling of physical tension. Impulses akin to electricity that pulse through me like lightening. A desire to punch something, kick out, scream even.

But I don't. I breathe and notice.

I notice that I am both highly physically stressed and deeply exhausted.

I can't lie in bed: the proximity of another makes me feel worse. So I get up, make a cup of tea.

I do some stretches, breathe, notice.

And then I am inexplicably crying.

Because I am sad.

Sad that I find it hard to see the joy in things.

Sad that there have been nearly thirty years of this.

Sad that I have this week read Virginia Woolf's suicide note to her husband where she admits that she cannot overcome the voices that torment her and can see no other way out.

But I am also hopeful.

I know the voices can be overcome. That there is a lot of science and research that backs this up.

I know that I need to keep going. To remember that there is a self inside me who needs to be nurtured and not silenced, criticised, hurt and punished. That I don't need to fear life.

I know that I don't need to put stones in my pockets and walk into the water, even if, at times, it might be tempting.

I need to keep going.

Posted on October 20, 2016

A White Dog.

A corner turned?

No formal exercise for three days. I am still alive.

A huge meal out last night where I ordered what I wanted to eat from the menu rather than what I thought would have least calories. I am still alive.

I have been for a stroll each day with husband and dogs. I have breathed, noticed.

I slept well last night.

I have a new white puppy and I am training her. She is called Forget Me Not.

She was hurt by her first owner. She was shouted at, hit and shut away. Sometimes I find her whimpering, trembling, locked in a state of distress and detached from me. When she gets like this she often runs mindlessly in circles as if she is running away from something. And she growls and nips.

But I am slowly retraining her.

When she gets upset, I hold her. I whisper in her ear:

You are loved.

When you see the other puppies and think they are better, happier, more deserving than you in their smart collars you are mistaken.

You deserve to be here as much as every other puppy in the world. And you should have a smart collar and wear it proudly and confidently.

And her breath slows and she relaxes.

And after that we run together and jump and dance on the sand and sing and bark for joy.

There are still bad days. But there are better days. And the bad days are getting less.

Any dog of any age can learn new tricks.

And with tricks come magic and sparkle.

Posted on October 28, 2016

Lessons.

A few months back a young person with whom I work was unable to overcome her mental health challenges and made a decision with unalterable consequences.

The fallout has been very difficult to handle and has left me feeling powerless and sad.

Could I have helped more/ done more/ shouted louder to get others to help?

Possibly, yes. But probably, no.

I have felt guilty, angry, sad. But now that I have had time to reflect, I feel that there is only one possible option.

To keep going with spreading the message of my story.

The message that, no matter how much others are there for us, listen to us and help us, the one person we need to make peace with is our self.

Posted on November 5, 2016

I have changed.

A small triumph this week amongst a lot of anxiety and struggle relating to work. Even some thoughts of stones in pockets and a desire to just escape.

A friend who I have not seen for a couple of months said 'I'd like to take you out for lunch, even though I know you don't eat lunch.'

'You're wrong there.' I said. "I do now. I have changed.'

Even saying that is a big thing for me. As I said it, I had a little shudder of panic, shame, disgust. But I ignored it and felt proud.

I have changed.

Posted on November 11, 2016

Life is not perfect.

So this has been an interesting week.

No less challenge at work than ever.

A catastrophic election result in the US.

The death of a legend.

A diagnosis of a minor but painful health condition.

And each of these brought been a wave crashing onto the shore. I have wept: the most over Trump and what that means.

But I have also sung my heart out in my choir, breathed deeply and felt ok. I have eaten well and bought energy packed smoothies and Eisberg instead of wine. And I am ok.

Nothing can hurt or stop me like it used to.

My mind is mine and I understand it.

"Life is not perfect. Bad things happen and we can't always control events around us. There are good feelings as well as bad. But we can have control over our thoughts and our actions if we understand, deeply, who we are and why we have behaved in certain ways in the past."

The Story of My Self.

Posted on November 19, 2016

A blip.

A blip this week.

Wednesday was a long day. Travelling and working out of the office and little time to stop and think. Lunch left at home and so nothing to eat after a light breakfast.

As I look back now I can see that I was high on hunger when I got to my 6 o' clock meeting. Slightly manic, talking too fast and light headed.

When I got home at 10pm, the signs were screaming out at anyone who might have been looking on objectively. My husband had made me supper but instead of sitting down, relaxing, eating, I walked straight through the door and began to wash up. I was irritable, hostile, critical..... Fearful.

And then I noticed. 'Sorry'. I said. I have not eaten all day. 'That's why I am grumpy'.

And I sat and ate.

And it was ok.

And I am ok.

Posted on December 11, 2016

Telling our stories and surviving.

This week, Michelle Thomson MP spoke in the House of Commons about her experience of being attacked as a 14 year-old as part of part of a debate on the UN's International Day for the Elimination of Violence Against Women.

Sky news reported:

Ms Thomson said her senses were "absolutely numbed", telling MPs: "Thinking about it now, 37 years later, I cannot remember hearing anything when I replay it in my mind."

Ms Thomson said she did not tell anyone about the attack at the time, saying she felt "ashamed".

She added: "I felt I was spoiled and impure and really felt revulsion towards myself.

"I, of course, then detached from the child up to then I had been."

She spoke of being a survivor, not a victim. She spoke of having told her family about the trauma and having moved on from it.

I sat in my car on hearing this story and cried. I cried for her and I cried for me and the 7-year old girl who detached from the child she had been and felt shame and revulsion.

But then I looked at her and I looked at me. Look at us. Strong, successful women who have not been broken and who prove that bad things can happen but that we can survive.

Telling the story is part of the survival process.

Posted on November 26, 2016

Sharing our secrets.

This week has brought a whole new wave of revelations about sexual abuse, this time in the world of football.

The scale is shocking and the resolution by politicians, leaders and those who work with children to ensure that historic events are not repeated is clear.

It is absolutely essential that those who perpetrate crimes against children are stopped and punished.

It is absolutely right that we review the safeguarding procedures of all bodies who have involvement with children.

But there will be children who may be silenced by the current level of exposure in the media. Children who know that nothing can be done to a perpetrator because he or she is dead. Children who fear that if they speak out they will become the focus of an attention that would be far worse than any distress and trauma caused by the original abuse.

I am a survivor who did not speak soon enough and suffered for years as a consequence. I have written my Story to show that recovery is possible.

But I urge those of us who work with children to make sure that we do not allow the current media circus to prevent us from educating sensitively and sensibly around abuse.

I would never have wanted punishment or a fuss. But I would have been helped by having someone to talk to, to help me feel ok. I would have been helped by reassurance that my life could be OK regardless of what had happened.

My Story tells why.

It will take you between 1 and 2 hours to read.

Please read it, share it.

Share the urgency. Share the hope.

Posted on December 5, 2016

Taking stock.

This week I have been reflecting. Girding my loins. Preparing for a fight ahead.

And heeding my own words.

Posted on December 17, 2016

To love and be loved.

I have lost weight.

I am not sure why. I haven't been trying. I have been eating sensibly and I have not been over-exercising.

Maybe it's because I have cut down on alcohol. Maybe it's because I had a cold. Maybe it's because work is insanely intense.

In spite of the fact that I know it shouldn't, it makes me feel good. I secretly love having a six pack. I secretly love having no stomach.

I secretly get a buzz from having cheekbones and from my clothes feeling loose.

It is shallow. It is hypocritical after all I have said and written. But it is true. And it is exhilarating.

However, last night I watched Graham Norton where the guests were the incredibly talented Nicole Kidman and Dawn French. And it made me think. Our talent is not related to our size or shape.

There is no better in being skinny.

I am tired and I am on the edge of falling into a low as we approach Christmas. But I won't.

I won't go back to where I was this time last year.

I am not going back there. I have worked too hard this year to let myself.

Over the next week I will eat, drink and allow myself to slow down, notice, appreciate and be merry. To survive and thrive.

To love and be loved.

Happy Christmas.

Posted on December 23, 2016

And finally home for the holidays.

I am exhausted but not beyond exhaustion.

I have managed a huge amount of challenge and yet remained calm and focussed.

Time now to switch off, recharge and relax.

Time to love my loved ones.

Time to eat, drink, be merry and not worry.

Time to have fun, dance and sing.

Time to celebrate how far I have come.

Time to re-read my own words and advice. To remember My Self and my story.

If you have come with me on my journey in 2016, I am hugely grateful to you.

You are amazing.

Together we are stronger.

Happy Christmas

You deserve to be happy and you can be.

If today, you are fearful, depressed, anxious, trying to avoid food or people, don't think it can't be different.

It can and you can make it so. I am living proof. This was my Christmas Day in 1987, aged 18:

"25th December

Well I have no excuse for not having written for two months other than being lazy. A lot has happened in actual fact but to cut a long story short it has been a very difficult time. I suppose the fact that I'm not home for Christmas is making me feel especially sad and pensive but to be quite honest I do wonder how I'm going to get through another eight months of this. Today I'm feeling a real mixture of emotions because although I feel terribly homesick and I miss home so much that it hurts I also know that I'm very lucky to be doing what I'm doing and having the experience as I am aged 18.

The good news is that I've lost a lot of weight and of got down to 120 pounds.

This holiday all I've eaten is vegetables but I can honestly say that I'm not hungry any more."

I have been mostly fearful of Christmas for the 29 years in between. Fearful or anxious or sad. I have hidden it well...and not so well.....

But this year I'm not those things. I'm grateful, joyous and very, very blessed.

Above all I am thankful for amazing writing by Emma Woolf, Tim O'Brien, Matt Haig and JK Rowling.

And for my amazing Twitter tribe.

Reading and writing have saved me and they can save you. And talking and loving and being kind to yourself and others.

I did it this year and you can too.

Do it. Now. Life is amazing and too precious to waste. Don't take as long as I did to find Your Self.

Happy Christmas.

With love from Nell xx

Posted on December 28, 2016

Read, reflect, write, recover, repeat.

Read, reflect, write, recover, repeat.

At the start of 2016 I was in a very different place.

I was going through the motions. I was acting happy. I was playing at success.

As I approached the new year, I decided something needed to change.

And slowly, I began to make changes. I started to tell people about my anxiety and depression. I wrote blog posts focusing on wellbeing and mental health.

I read and did internal work based on 'Inner Story' by Dr Tim O'Brien, 'Letting Go' by Emma Woolf and 'Reasons to Stay Alive' by Matt Haig.

In July, however, I faced a bit of a crisis. Exhausted and despondent, I broke down in front of my parents and brother and told them that I was fed up with pretending, that I knew I couldn't really ever be ok and that it wasn't worth the effort any more. That I was a failure as a parent and wife.

And then my brother said the words that saved me. He told me that he was utterly confident that I could and would feel better but that I just had to take some time to explore my self and unlearn some of the negative behaviours and thought patterns that I had developed over years. 'It's simple', he said. 'You just need to take some time and space to understand what happened to you.'

He suggested therapy but I decided there and then that the therapist I needed was inside me.

And writing was my therapy.

Last summer I began to write my story.

Reading, writing and reflecting have all helped me to arrive at a point where I understand myself.

As 2017 approaches, I urge you to try this road to recovery.

Because we deserve to be happy. We deserve to be loved and nurtured.

We deserve to live.

Posted on January 3, 2017

Unhappy New Year

I feel sad.

The holiday is over.

Loved ones left behind until another visit.

A wrench.

A small heartbreak.

I feel tired. Even after a break, a broken night's sleep last night and middle-of-the night terrors have left me exhausted.

The positivity and optimism circulating Twitter are not resonating.

And perhaps more significant than anything, another terrible piece of news has left me feeling powerless, guilt-ridden and incredibly sad.

A while back I wrote this:

https://nellflowersblog.wordpress.com/2016/10/28/lessons/

Today I read it again and wonder.

Are my words hollow after all?

Do I need to give up this fight and leave it to others who are more robust and better qualified?

One thing is certain: I need to spend some time reflecting before I make any decisions. And I need some support from others too.

There is no sense at present in which this is a Happy New Year.

Posted on January 6, 2017

On death and life.

The last week has been overshadowed by death. The death of a friend's parent. The death of my dad's friend. The death of a young person I worked with.

It has been a week of grief.

Death has for many years petrified and pre-occupied me and I have touched on this in my writing.

This week on the radio I listened to something about trauma which touched on the idea that experiencing trauma can rob you of a sense that life is secure and safe. I know that for me, this was the case and that because I could not and did not talk about what had happened to me as child, I gradually lost my childish sense of optimism and hope.

Having had my innocence taken away, I became hugely fearful of death as the ultimate taker……but perversely, in the depths of my illness, I later also wondered whether it might be the only answer to finding peace and relief from my shame and self-hatred.

This week, I am in a different place. The deaths that have occurred have made me feel hugely sad but they have not made me fearful. They have reminded me of how much I want to live.

And how much I want the children I work with to know that death is never an answer to our problems.

No matter how bad you feel, you can feel better.

No matter how sad you feel, you can feel better.

No matter how mad you feel, you can feel better.

Death can take everything away but can also remind us of how much there is to celebrate about living.

Posted on January 15th, 2016

No words.

Exhausted and wordless from giving words of comfort to others.

There is only sadness and my tears won't stop right now.

But life does and must go on.

Posted on January 21, 2017

Lucky.

This week I am feeling lucky.

Things have been difficult: work-wise, head-wise and family-wise.

A shock piece of news last week knocked me for six.

But lots of good things have happened and I have managed to navigate the hard things by breathing, focusing and allowing myself to feel but not be overwhelmed by the feelings.

At the end of twelve-hour work days, there has been wonderful food on the table, love and support at home.

I am incredibly blessed.

Posted on January 27, 2017

That frustrating dance....

One step forward, two steps back.

Life is a frustrating dance.

You think things are going ok. Almost allow yourself to admit it. And then you get smashed down again. Like that moment when you are swimming and wave-surfing and the ocean takes your feet and you are swirling, out of control, unable to breathe and wondering if you will come up again.

I have been reminded once again of mortality. The C word has rocked our family world.

So inevitable, really, when you look at the statistics. So many contemporaries have survived it or been taken. But never so close-by before.

Using the word, it feels wrong in my mouth. In that sentence. About him. I never thought.

The not knowing is the worst. How much. How far. Another scan. Another week of waiting.

Tears keep sneaking out, just when I think I am in control.

In the bathroom. In the supermarket carpark. In my car.

Hope and positivity are the only options. And a celebration and savouring of every precious moment.

Because who knows?

Posted on February 3, 2017

Hope again.

The tide comes in and goes out.

After rain there are rainbows.

The bad stuff is still there but it feels less raw.

Work has been a good distraction.

Many of the children I work with have survived much worse and their resilience is an inspiration.

I am keeping going.

Posted on February 10, 2017

Saying it again.

It has been a long week. I have been incredibly busy at work. There have been lots of positives.

Also this week I have been very affected by watching ITV's 'Unforgiven' which featured a plot about child sex abuse.

Difficult emotions have been stirred. I have been reminded of things I would rather forget.

But I am strong. I have survived.

Posted on February 18, 2017

Wondering.

What are my words worth?

I have been reflecting this week on whether to continue with my writing.

I guess I had hoped that more people might have responded to it; that I might have inspired and encouraged more readers to explore their own stories and realise that we can recover from childhood trauma by recognising the things that have hurt us and taking time to understanding our behaviours and vulnerabilities; that my Twitter following might have grown and that more people might have approved of me; that Matt Haig or Brené Brown might have given me just one like or retweet.

Maybe the writing isn't very good.

Maybe the format doesn't work.

Maybe I have nothing new or original to contribute.

Maybe I should just give up.

But maybe, just maybe, it is good enough. Maybe I am good enough. Maybe the need for approval from others is part of what I need to learn to overcome if I am going to continue on my journey to find my Self.

So, please feel free to read and share my journey if it interests or helps you.

If not, I'll be here, writing and journeying alone but not giving up.

How honest?

I have a dilemma.

A young relative is struggling. The way I struggled. The questions and anxieties about the meaning of life. The low mood that is hard to shake.

Sometimes the wanting not to be here.

He thinks that no-one gets him. That no-one will ever understand and that it will never be better.

But I do understand. I do know that it can be better if he works at it, faces some of the difficult questions and accepts that lots of us have been there.

I understand better than anyone

I have given him 'Reasons to stay Alive', even though he is just 13, because he is a thinker and a reader.

I have told him that I understand, that I have struggled. But I am wondering whether I should share my story with him. My fear is that he needs me to be strong and that if he sees my vulnerability, he may panic, feel that there is no hope because of his genetics and upbringing.

I wrote my story because I want to help others avoid taking 40 years to feel better.

But is this too close to home for my young friend who is so incredible but feeling so awful?

If you read this and have ideas, I'd love to hear from you.

Thank you.

Posted on March 11, 2017

A Blip.

I have struggled this last week and I have reverted to some unhelpful behaviours. But I am not broken and I will get back on track.

So, no new words today.

Posted on March 17, 2017

I am enough.

I write, therefore I am.

This week has been amazing.

I have worked incredibly hard. I have taken care of myself. I have eaten well and avoided too much alcohol, though I did give in last night and share a Thursday night bottle of wine with my husband. But I have not beaten myself up about it.

I have written lots.

I have also pondered whether to make a big career move but have decided against it.

I am enough. I have spent my life trying to prove myself to others and to myself, always hoping that the next move, the next promotion would make me feel satisfied.

But I know that a promotion now would not be right. Not for me, not for my family.

I am enough. I have a great job where I have the power to help young people reach their potential and find contentment.

What else would I need?

Posted on March 25, 2017

On wanting to live.

There has been a lot of reference to suicide in my life this week. By young people I work with, by Twitter friends and in various articles I have read.

I attended the debrief on the suicide of a young person a while back. It was clinical, formal and 'necessary' but I found myself wondering how on earth we had ever got to the position of needing it.

And I sat there, wondering how many of the others round the table really understood what it feels like to want to die.

I know I have and my diary entries in my story remind me of that.

I was lucky that I stepped back from the brink of anorexia. I was lucky that I didn't actually drive my car off the road. I was lucky that I didn't drown. At the time, the desperation and impulsiveness were so great that things may have worked out differently.

I wanted to ask the people in the debrief room if they had ever wanted not to be here. I imagine that they hadn't. The jokey policeman. The sharp suited social worker. The highly intelligent paediatrician.

But what would they have thought of the calm, articulate and compassionate educator who spoke so knowledgeably about the impact of adverse childhood experiences, of neglect and of needing to improve our first and second tier responses to distress and dysfunctional behaviour.

They didn't see Nell or know her story. What would have happened if they had? My fear is that suddenly they would have become suspicious of her vulnerability, have re-framed their opinion of her, have judged her differently.

But maybe not.

What would happen if I shared her story with the young people I work with?

Because I am not suicidal now. I want to live. Because life is amazing. And since writing and analysing my story, I know that the anxiety, sadness and negativity that I still have to battle are getting less with every day and every word I write.

Because those things came about when someone hurt me. And they have been there for too long because I did not take time or space to understand them.

Now I do. I know that the only way we can stop people wanting to die is to help them find the time and space to understand themselves and their story; as teachers and parents we must give all children that help, time and space.

Posted on April 2, 2017

Shut up.

I have been in a bad place today. Sad, angry, blaming, crying and frantically trying to keep busy.

A typical start of a holiday for me.

Not fair on the ones I love and live with. Not fair on my lovely children and husband who deserve better.

But above all, not fair on my Self.

I recognise the voices in my head who are winning because I am tired and a bit low and because it is time for me to take a break. The voices who tell me that relaxing is indulgent, that I don't deserve it and that I need to be punished.

The same voices who used to tell me that eating was indulgent and that pushing myself to exercise excessively was ok.

But they can shut right up.

I have worked incredibly hard this term and things have not been easy. Huge problems at work. Interpersonal issues. Family illness.

Financial worries.

But none of those will kill me. I can survive all of those things.

What could kill me are those voices. Because if I don't stop for a bit now, I will become ill.

So now, instead of mowing the lawn/ typing a report/doing another load of washing/ saving the world, I am going to sit in the garden with a beer and listen to the birds sing and the wind blow. I might read my book. I might paint my nails. I might design my next tattoo. But I might not.

Life is beautiful and I will keep living it. The ugly, critical voices are not welcome here.

Posted on April 8, 2017

It's going to be ok.

Last week I wrote about the need to switch off and silence the damaging voices in my head.

I have to confess that I have not entirely succeeded and, a week in to my spring break and I am struggling a bit.

I feel tired. I feel like crying. I feel cross. I feel like a failure in most parts of my life (friend, mum, wife and teacher). I feel ugly. An imposter. A not real person. A misfit. I am desperately worried about what is happening in the world and the fact that I can't control it.

I am obsessed with dog hair. Everywhere. Driving me distracted.

I have a project to complete for work which I need to spend the rest of the holidays on and I can think of little else.

The sun is shining. I have a beautiful home and family and a good job. But I want to curl up under the covers and to wake up feeling better.

I have been here before.

I have come out of it before.

The answers?

Books- Frazzled by Ruby Wax and Reasons to Stay Alive by Matt Haig.

Hugs.

Mindfulness meditation.

The Story of My Self.

Maybe a bit of hoovering to tackle some of the dog hair mountain.

It's going to be ok.

Posted on April 14, 2017

Bravery and a revelation.

Last week I took a bold step.

I shared The Story of My Self with a friend who has known me for nearly thirty years.

She knew me through some of my darkest days and yet, at the time, she did not know the reality of what I was going through because I could not share it with anyone.

After she read my Story, she wrote me a letter. She told me that it had moved her hugely, made her cry and shocked her in terms of what it revealed about my internal struggles over the years.

She explained some of her own insecurities and self-doubts and reminded me that we are all connected by our struggles and attempts to face the challenges that life throws at us.

But she also outlined one important difference between us, relating to the pervasive sense of guilt and worthlessness which I feel and she does not.

She does not.

True, she has days where she may feel a bit rubbish, down or doubtful but fundamentally she does not feel a sense of worthlessness or guilt.

Why did that surprise me? Because until she said it, I would have assumed that she does. That everyone does. That everyone faces a daily struggle of pretending.

That if everyone was just a bit more honest, we'd all admit to it.

That all of us who share the positive quotes, talk about optimism and contentment are secretly hiding the fact that it is all a lie.

That most of us don't really like ourselves.

People have told me before that my feelings are not the norm: my mum, counsellors, experts who write books and must therefore surely know.

But I have always suspected that they are wrong, that they are just pretending, that the world is so full of awfulness that life can only ever be about putting on a brave face and fighting the pervasive negative feelings and anxieties on a daily basis.

But my friend has shown me that my suspicion is wrong.

And it makes sense really, doesn't it? Because if the life force in the majority of human beings was not strong, if the fire of joy and passion was but burning brightly, we would not be here, would we?

My friend says that she wishes she could help me to stop feeling guilty and worthless.

But she has helped me. Her honest words on response to my writing have helped me to see that there is still work for me to do.

I am hugely blessed and grateful.

The seven year old me was loveable.

The seven year old me had nothing to feel guilty about.

The seven year old me was playful, contented and full of optimism.

The work continues in getting her back.

Posted on April 21, 2017

That's enough.

I have had a great week.

I have achieved a lot, looked after myself and practised a lot of self-care: gentle exercise, good food, enough sleep and no alcohol.

I have made some real progress at work. There have been challenges but I have found solutions.

Life is good. I am doing well and I feel positive about myself and my achievements.

That's enough.

Posted on April 30, 2017

Finding strength.

I have been incredibly busy this week. A huge work deadline is looming and it has meant phenomenally long days and short nights.

I don't like to be this busy or pressured as I know that the stress it creates is bad for my health and leaves me short-tempered and prone to falling into a low mood. I also struggle horribly with the voices in my head who tell me that I am bound to fail, that my whole life depends on this and that I am not up to the job.

However, I am managing to retain a centre of calm and perspective in the midst of it all.

How?

By connecting with others who make me feel loved and valued and who are able to remind me that I have been here before and that I can.

By remembering that it is not the task that is the problem but the voices in my head that seek to derail and sabotage me. I know from writing The Story of My Self that these voices are not the real me and that they are voices of defence and habit. But they are not welcome. When I was 18 and at my lowest ebb, I was offered a job in a garden centre, bedding out seedlings. I could not do it as I was so wracked with doubt and fear ….yet I was the girl who, six months before had passed the most challenging of exams, was due to go to a prestigious university and who had the world at her feet.

The task is not the issue. The issue is needing to manage and know my Self, my emotions, my strengths and my weaknesses.

By practising mindfulness. Breathing. Noticing and writing down three things for which to be grateful every single morning. Remembering that life has no definitive meaning but is infinitely meaningful when we chose to live it purposefully and positively.

And remembering the words of some great thinkers:

'Il n'y a qu'un problème philosophique vraiment sérieux : c'est le suicide.'

Albert Camus

"Once a person is determined to help themselves, there is nothing that can stop them."

And

'It always seems impossible until it's done.'

Nelson Mandela.

I feel exhausted and exhilarated. A bit broken but strong.

Posted on May 5, 2017

Blessed.

All in all a brilliant week.

A friend from childhood read my story and was moved and inspired by it. She also passed it on to a friend whose daughter has anorexia and she in turn found it very helpful.

If I have helped just one person with my writing then it will have been worth it.

I have connected with incredible people via the Internet but also in the real world.

Family visited at the weekend and I was able to share the joy of my life in the beautiful place where I live with my husband and children.

I have made great strides forward at work by being brave and having moral courage.

I have celebrated week three with no alcohol.

I have eaten well and exercised (almost) every day and forgiven myself when I have not.

I have practised mindfulness even in the most stressful moments.

I feel blessed.

Posted on May 14, 2017

I have had enough of myself this week.

Don't panic. I am not planning on doing anything drastic but I am a bit exhausted from being me.

The hundreds of thoughts and questions that whizz around in my brain during every waking hour are what make me productive and effective but sometime I just want them to stop.

The physical restlessness in me is what means that I never miss my step count target.

The intense sensitivity and hyper-vigilance I experience means that I never inadvertently over-eat or let things slip.

All the things about me that are positive and help me to be the me who does and achieves... but they are exhausting.

I need to go back to Mindfulness.

By a strange co-incidence, Danny Penman followed me on Twitter this week and it reminded me: back to the breath. Back to the real me. Back to the Self that is not my thoughts and internal voices and impulses.

I can do this.

Posted on May 19, 2017

I am and I am not Three Girls.

This week I watched the BBC drama Three Girls, the story of the appalling mishandling of the Rochdale child exploitation cases.

It was heart-breaking, anger-inducing but above all inspiring because (spoiler alert) in the end, right triumphed and we saw the incredible strength and power of young women who overcame everything to ensure justice for themselves and other abused children.

It is incredibly uncomfortable viewing. But incredibly important.

Important because it restores faith in the fact that we should never give up fighting if we know that something is wrong. We can all be and should aspire to be Sara Rowbotham and Maggie Oliver. As educators we need to remember this: we can be the turnaround adult in the life of a Holly or an Amber or a Ruby, no matter how much they might be let down by others or the system.

Important because it shows that experiencing abuse and trauma is not a death sentence. It is completely unsurprising that Holly becomes an alcoholic, suicidal and nearly throws her life away. But it is also crucially important that she survives and thrives, that she fights against the shame (not guilt) that has been inflicted upon her and that she keeps on going.

After I eventually managed to talk about what someone had done to me when I was seven years old, one of the responses I got was to be told that things like that happen to most people at some point or another.

In retrospect, I think that this was one of the most unhelpful things for me because it meant that I tried to ignore it and carry on without addressing the impact that the abuse had had on me. In 'The Story of My Self', I have written:

'Some bad things happened to me once. On the scale of it, they weren't really bad things and other people might have experienced them and not reacted as I did. But for me, they were traumatic and resulted in me developing ways of trying to protect myself against trauma in the future.'

It took me too long to acknowledge the impact of what had happened to me and I can't help feeling that the underplaying of it by a key adult exacerbated that.

Child sexual abuse is never ok and should never be dismissed as 'something that happens'.

It does not only happen to 'certain types of children'. I am Holly and Amber and Ruby.

As adults we need to be vigilant, protect children and talk to them so that they know what is ok and what is not.

But we also need to be honest when abuse has happened and help children to understand that they are still lovable, blameless and full of potential.

I am Sara and I am Maggie and as adults, we all need to be them.

Posted on May 27, 2017

Back to love.

I am excessively tired.

I have worked too hard in order to meet a huge deadline and the elation of meeting that deadline has been extinguished by exhaustion.

So this weekend I will rest.

I am excessively sad. The Manchester bombing, the stories of some of the children I work with, the fact that my own child struggles with low mood in spite of all my best efforts have left me tearful and raw, lacking in resilience and hope.

So this weekend I will reflect.

I am excessively angry. With that bomber. With adults who take on the privilege of working with young lives but don't accept the responsibility that goes with it. With myself for breaking all my wellbeing rules and allowing myself to get here. With everyone and everything.

So this weekend I will look deep inside and find forgiveness.

Back to the breath.

Back to the moment.

Back to love.

On rejection.

I am feeling a bit down. I had been hoping that someone would take on my book idea but today I got a rejection.

I know well enough that writing and getting published is a huge challenge and that the likelihood of it happening is a pipe dream.

But if I consider again why I write, I know that it really isn't about fame or fortune.

I write because I want to spread a message:

You can suffer abuse and trauma and recover.

You can beat anorexia.

You can find the beauty in life even if you have been to places where you thought you never would.

A few people have read my writing and gained hope from it.

That is enough.

I am enough.

I am more than enough.

Posted on June 5, 2017

A message to my younger self.

Bad things happen but you worrying about them won't make them stop happening.

Nuclear weapons could and might wipe out the world. So shout your slogans and march your marches. Support those Greenham women and do your best to make Reagan and Gorbachev listen. But don't let the fear take away your sleep. Don't forget that the world is full of peace loving flower and rainbow children like you.

You were hurt by someone who should have known better. You did nothing wrong. You must feel no guilt or shame. And you must talk about what happened so that we can love and help you, soothe your pain and dry your tears.

The IRA has taken too many lives and needs to be stopped. But their actions are the actions of a misguided minority. You do not need to worry anxiously about your loved ones every minute of every day.

You are so loveable and you do not need to live in despair and pessimism. The world is a good place with bad moments, not the other way around.

 Let's repeat these words to the children of today, to suit their context, so that they may live in the light.

Taking the wheel again.

Things have slipped. I am back in the spiral of being driven, rather than being in the driver's seat.

Work has become all-consuming and I have realised that I can't go a day without exercising, even when I am at my most exhausted.

Life has become devoid of joy and tinged with feelings of negativity that won't be shifted.

Nothing too bad but time to take stock.

I think I am responding to a difficult time of late; at work, personally and in the world.

Nothing catastrophic.

So:

I will not work this weekend, except for a limited slot on Sunday afternoon.

I will have a day off exercise tomorrow.

I will not skip eating as a consequence of the day off!

I will practice mindfulness and remember the words of Dr Danny Penman on Twitter:

"Your normal ways of dealing with uncomfortable thoughts, feelings & emotions may not be in your best interests. Breathe before reacting."

I am blessed.

Posted on June 17, 2017

Honesty and authenticity.

These are words which trouble me.

Because if I am honest, I am still unable to be.

The woman you read about and support and offer your compassion to here is not the woman I am in day to day life, with the people who see me in the flesh. Some of my closest friends and family know Nell but most don't.

Although I have written about needing to overcome stigma, to speak openly and to accept that mental illness is no different to physical illness, I still hide.

Although I advocate the need for us to talk openly and honestly with children about abuse and trauma so that they can live without shame, I still hide.

Why?

Because I am still scared that you will judge me. That as soon as I tell you, you will forget all the wonderful, inspirational things that I have done and can do and that you will see me through different eyes.

That you will become suspicious of as a professional, put my application to one side when I apply for your job and see me as unreliable.

That you will stop seeing me, your mother, as a role model and be disappointed in me.

Because these things have happened just a little bit to me in the past when I have been honest, either through necessity or choice.

There were the jobs I am sure I did not get because I had put 'previous eating disorder' on my application. There were the friends and lovers who made a quick excuse and exit when I told them just a little bit of my truth.

I am in huge admiration of those I know who write as themselves, appear publicly and demonstrate genuine authenticity.

I tell myself that I will too, when I win the lottery or retire and don't have anything to lose any more.

But for now I continue to hide. Please forgive me and don't judge me for that.

Posted on June 18, 2017

For Father's Day

My dad is a little bit broken.

A couple of tiny things have grown inside and are causing all sorts of havoc.

And all of a sudden we are using the word cancer.

They are trying to fix it.

With poison.

Once a month through a tube, straight into his arm. Sitting in the hospital for a couple of hours.

And then tablets. Tablets. Tablets.

Tens a day.

It makes him so very ill. The cure that causes more illness than the illness.

Horrible tummy aches.

Painful skin.

Freezing.

Not able to breathe.

Eating for comfort. Rice pudding. Custard. Peaches.

Sleeping and sleeping and sleeping. Like a baby. So restful to observe. And yet somehow heart-breaking..

But between the naps, still his lovely self. Dad. Grandad.

Coming for (shorter) walks. Joking and laughing. Loving us as much as ever.

Looking with those expressive eyes that remind me so much of his mum. Grandma. Great-Grandma.

Occasional moments of fear in those eyes.

The eyes that helped take away my fears. Re-assuring. Soothing. Calming.

And now we wait for the next results.

Hoping above everything that the things will have receded.

That we will begin to use the word 'remission' as part of our vocabulary.

That my dad will be fixed.

That hope will make it so.

Posted on June 24, 2017

Weather.

I have announced to my husband that I want to put the house on the market and move back down to where I grew up.

My dad is poorly and we are too far away.

My garden is overrun with weeds.

No one at school appreciates me and my efforts to change the culture over the last year have fallen in vain ears. The children are unhappy.

We have made no friends here and all the people who 'get' me live miles away.

I am exhausted and sad and life is so unfair.

The house is a tip and the washing is not done.

I work and work and work and still we have no money.

I can't do it all.

I then I hear myself say. "But maybe not."

I burst into tears.

I breathe for a while.

And I remember.

I have the three best, most loving human beings right here with me.

I have felt like people have never 'got' me, anywhere I have lived. Some of that has been about me keeping them at arm's length.

I live in an amazing place.

I have an amazing job and this year, I have done it incredibly well.

I have incredible support from friends I have made online. I don't care how 'real' they are. They are real to me.

I have choices.

When I was about 19, I drove to Cornwall with my brother and his friends and the song 'Weather with you' by Crowded House was almost constantly on the radio.

It annoyed the hell out of him and I could never work out why. Looking back, I think it is because it contains a truth which is massively empowering but also almost too much to bear.

I could go anywhere but my weather goes with me.

Now, as I listen to the blackbird sing outside my window and hear the clock tick, the storm abates.

The rain is stopping and the sun is coming out.

Posted on June 29, 2017

10% braver.

Tomorrow I stop for the holidays.

I am exhausted but also irrepressibly excited.

I have lots of wonderful adventures planned, which will include catching up with old friends, new friends and some good old-fashioned sea-side holiday fun.

I will get to see my lovely dad and understand from closer at-hand how his illness is impacting on him.

I have a feeling that I will shed many tears.

When I saw him this time year, I never guessed that we would be where we are just a year on.

But all we can do is hope and love.

Last year I set about writing my Story. I am so proud that I did so and that since, I have followed it up with almost a year's worth of weekly blogs to chart my progress.

The connections that I have made through writing have given me huge amounts of confidence and support.

I still have days full of anxiety but the days of despair that I used to feel are far and few between.

I love my life.

I no longer live in fear of the ghosts of my past because I have named them and owned them.

It is forty years this summer since I experienced the trauma that took away my innocence.

It is thirty years this summer since my mental wellbeing really began to unravel.

But in a year I have achieved a huge amount of healing, with the support of wonderful people who exist in my virtual world.

I am Nell Flowers and I am not.

My 10% braver this next year will be to connect her with more of those in my non-virtual world.

I am not going to wait until I win the lottery. I have all riches I need.

Posted on July 1, 2017

Round or square?

Last night I played a game at the train station.

As we sat on the bench and watched people pass, I tried to work out which passer-by was most like me. Not in the sense of complete physical resemblance but in the sense of type, aura, energy.

Am I the together business woman with perfect sleek bob and immaculate suit, free of creases and dog hair?

Of course not. That is how I always hoped I might be one day but have never managed.

Am I the confident, alternative but cool DM wearing, striding bohemian type?

No. That would be another aspiration never achieved.

Am I the woman with hunched shoulders, badly dyed hair and a world-weary look? A bit scruffy. Lacking in togetherness? Out of kilter?

That is how I feel. That is how I have always felt, I think.

Different. An outsider. Uneasy. Disconnected from my physical self

But I wonder how all of those women who fall under my scrutiny actually feel on the inside?

Maybe not together?

Maybe not confident?

Maybe not world-weary?

I have a sneaking suspicion that lots of us feel different in the inside than our external appearance and image might indicate.

And I have a sneaking suspicion that if more of us had the courage to admit to this, we'd all feel more connection with each other and the world.

I read this by the wonderful @betateacher today:

https://betateacherblog.wordpress.com/2017/06/28/round-pegs/amp/

I think that more of us may have more in common with Michael and Nigel than we might think. That more of us are round than square.

That if we could encourage each other to lose some of our sharp corners, we'd all find the world a bit more accepting, kinder, compassionate.

Maybe I'm wrong. What do you think?

My journey into light.

The story of my journey.

A year ago, almost to the day, I sat crying with my parents and brother at the dining table in my family home.

I had everything. Two children who make my heart burst with pride, a keeper of a husband, an incredible job in education, a beautiful home in a stunning location, the love of my family.

But I sat and cried because I felt desperately sad inside.

And then came the catalyst that propelled me into the journey which I have taken this year and which has been a slow journey from darkness into light.

'You don't need to feel like this. It is obvious why you do, after what happened to you when you were seven, but you can feel better. You just need to face up to it and talk about it. It's simple. You just need to take some time and space to understand what happened to you. Life can get better.'

And with that, something shifted. Hearing my brother talk out loud about the thing that has hung over me for forty years was like a shift in the space-time continuum and suddenly I could see that what he had said made perfect sense.

I decided to write the Story of My Self.

I got out the diaries, letters and writing that help to pull together the pieces of that story and I connected them together, reflecting and analysing as I did.

As I wrote, I also read and found the words of four key voices inspired me to keep going:

Matt Haig

Dr Tim O Brien

Emma Woolf

JK Rowling.

And in writing, I began truly to heal.

Taking time to stop, to see, to realise that all the things I know, as a teacher and therapist, about how to help and heal other children are the things that will finally help and heal me.

Through writing, I shaped and developed my mantra:

'Life is not perfect. Bad things happen and we can't always control events around us. There are good feelings as well as bad. But we can have control over our thoughts and our actions if we understand, deeply, who we are and why we have behaved in certain ways in the past.'

In August, I put my Story out into the world. The trepidation and anxiety that went with that were considerable but I did it anyway and slowly began to use social networks to share it.

And the sharing has enabled me to connect, be supported by and support others in way that was unimaginable to me until I did it.

You can try (as some have) to tell me that these connections are not real, that these relationships are shallow, that I am replacing human connection with false, electronic pseudo-attachment.

But these connections have saved me over the past year. I do not write that lightly.

I am someone who could never previously have talked to people in the room with me about the things I have shared through writing and virtual communication. But because I have made connections virtually, I am beginning to get braver in the real world.

How many of us misfits and outsiders have stood in a room full of people and felt completely detached and alone?

But here, in this world, I have found my tribe, I have found kindness, I have found love.

It might not work for you. If so, don't do it.

It has not been an easy year by any means: there have been almost unbearable situations at work, personal challenges relating to family and dilemmas that in the past would have sent me into a tailspin of anxiety, depression and addictive behaviours.

But as I sit here in the sunshine (with just a few showers) of my parents' garden, forty years on, I am ok. I am ok because of you, reading this. And I hope that maybe you might be a little bit more ok because of me.

Thank you.

Posted on July 8, 2017

This life.

That life:

Where you never feel tired;

Where you never feel upset;

Where your dad never gets ill;

Where your child never feels anxious;

Where you have enough money;

Where you experience perfect love;

Where you feel satisfied and calm all the time;

Stop waiting for it.

Live instead in this life:

Where your tiredness tells you that you need to rest;

Where being upset moves you to action;

Where your dad's illness brings you closer to him;

Where your child's anxiety makes you understand her better;

Where you value the money you have;

Where you love the imperfections;

Where you can breathe out all of the dissatisfaction and breathe in and find calm:

As you notice the sun

As you catch a feather

As you hear the birds sing

As you love this life.

Posted on July 14, 2017

Moments

I am feeling rested at last.

After a while off work, I had begun to wonder whether I would: relentless exhaustion, no matter how much I slept; a lowness of mood and at the same time an inability to stop thoughts and worries buzzing in my head; tummy ache, a sore throat, headaches.

But at last things feel better.

I have spent really important time with my family and realised how loved I am and how much love I feel.

I have eaten well and not allowed myself to feel guilty.

I have walked, swum and enjoyed being outside.

I have meditated, written and connected with amazing people through Twitter.

I am facing up to the bad stuff too: my dad's illness which is breaking my heart; my dissatisfaction with work; the increasingly worrying situation relating to climate change. I know that these are things beyond my control and that in the past they would have led me to try and exert control in other aspects of my life to help me cope.

But not now.

I heard the wonderful Matt Haig speak on radio 4 yesterday and have reflected since on two important points that he made:

1. Pessimism can be as untrustworthy as optimism.

2. We must learn to be in the present moment.

I am still learning. I don't expect ever to stop learning.

For me, learning and writing go hand in hand and this week I have written some thoughts on the week.

Monday

Another start

Another opportunity

Full of hope, magic and mystery.

Seize it.

Tuesday

Take a breath

Notice a week started but with so much still to come

The possibly hard edge of Monday

gone

And now a chance to focus, tackle, achieve.

Choose Day. What will the rest of the week be?

Wednesday

The middle for some.

But not for all.

The non-teachers.

Those with Saturday school.

The part-timers.

Those on holiday where days lack definition.

But for all

A chance to stop

Reflect on the days gone

Plan for those to come.

Wedding past and future.

Thursday.

So close to the weekend yet not there yet.

Sometimes close to an end of term, too.

But worth remembering that weekdays and workdays bring security and stability to some.

That weekends and holidays are not longed-for by all.

Blessed are those who love both the week and its end.

Friday.

A day to look back and celebrate achievements

Or forgive yourself and others for things gone awry.

There is undeniably that feeling, whether it is the week's end or not.

Five to five, Crunchie, a celebratory hashtag.

Find peace.

Finish.

And once again the weekend.

What will it bring?

Who knows?

For now, I will live the present.

With my dad.

In the moment.

Because who knows how many more moments we have?

Epilogue

So, were I to lay this story and evidence in front of a therapist, psychologist, psychiatrist, there would probably be some fairly obvious conclusions to be drawn.

I was a happy child with energy, ambition, strong attachments and a secure sense of self. Aged 7, I experienced a trauma that led me to develop a sense of guilt, fear and a feeling that the world was a scary place and not to be trusted.

I created psychological mechanisms for dealing with this that involved rituals and an inner monologue of shame and guilt but was still ultimately in a safe place where my family and friends continued to provide strong attachments and love. I had doubts and anxieties but probably not anything drastically different to those of a typical adolescent.

Aged 17 I went away for a holiday job and away from home. I experienced my first bout of depression and anxiety. Aged 18 I fell in love and had my heart broken. I went away again, far from home, far from my secure attachments, and fell apart.

I can hardly remember the few years after that and only the diary evidence serves as proof of who and what I briefly became.

There are any number of books that will tell you that anorexia is a difficult condition to address. Although it has a clear psychological element, the complications caused by the effects of starvation on the brain and physiology are hard to unpick.

Dieting is about becoming obsessed with food and calories but then starvation creates more food obsession and pre-occupation. The Minnesota Starvation experiment back in 1945 showed that the effects of starvation on male adults included pre-occupation with food, depression and anxiety and social isolation.

Some argue that engaging in any type of therapy with someone who is starving is pointless. I can only note that my diaries do not evidence much hope of real desire for recovery until I had begun to eat and gain weight.

But why, today, do I still have get a buzz by missing lunch? Why do I experience panic at the thought of missing exercise or having to eat something 'out of the ordinary?' Have my neurological pathways been altered for ever as a result of my early trauma and defences, my disordered eating and thinking? I would like to think not and embrace recent thinking that brain plasticity means that we can re-create pathways and move on.

But I guess that looking at it rationally and from a distance of nearly 40 years, it is not surprising that the recovery and undoing of the rituals and pathways has taken and will take time.

Matt Haig has written the best, most wonderful and readable analysis of depression that I have ever read in 'Reasons to stay Alive' and I keep returning to his book. He unpicks the complexity of why an individual (in this case himself) may end up suffering depression and points to the idea that the perfect storm often comes when certain factors collide. Physical habits such as excessive drinking; a naturally introspective personality; a tendency to question and overthink; exhaustion; the pressures of life in the twenty-first century: these may be the factors that, when all present simultaneously, allow the illness to slip between the cracks and get a hold.

This resonates a great deal with me. I don't think that one thing caused my life to fall apart in quite such a drastic way when it did.

And I don't think that there could have been an easy fix; nor is there still.

But although I knew what I needed to do so many times in the past, the reality of doing it is harder.

Even today I'd do well to heed the words of my 'Marianne' alter ego. Or certainly the wise rules for university written by my parents. And more than anything the advice I give to others in my own blogs.

If we humans could take advice or take a pill and make things better instantly then of course we would. By now, we'd have fixed it all, learnt from the mistakes of others and sorted it so that no-one ever got to the point of taking his or her life.

It is complex. Life is complex. It has been ever so; literature and music have the complexity of life and living at their heart. The irony is that I dismissed the study of literature so easily at university when I should have realised that it tells stories that need to be told to help us understand life.

Shakespeare gave us Hamlet, over 400 years ago:

"To be, or not to be: that is the question:

Whether 'tis nobler in the mind to suffer

The slings and arrows of outrageous fortune,

Or to take arms against a sea of troubles,

And by opposing end them? To die: to sleep;

No more; and by a sleep to say we end

The heart-ache and the thousand natural shocks

That flesh is heir to, 'tis a consummation

Devoutly to be wish'd. To die, to sleep;

To sleep: perchance to dream: ay, there's the rub;

For in that sleep of death what dreams may come

When we have shuffled off this mortal coil,

Must give us pause: there's the respect

That makes calamity of so long life;"

400 years ago. You might think that by now, with the vast amount of research and psychological and medical progress that has occurred since, we'd have a universal answer to life and happiness. But we don't.

Questions of life and death abound throughout writing, art and music. I could quote endlessly but the evidence is there.

Matt Haig writes, of books:

'They were, in and of themselves, reasons to stay alive. Every book written is the product of a human mind in a particular state. Add all the books together and you get the end sum of humanity. Every time I read a great book I felt I was reading a kind of map, a treasure map, and the treasure I was being directed to was in actual fact myself.'

Life is complex.

We are both animal and human.

We are both conscious and unconscious.

We both love and hate.

We both live and die.

We both marry and divorce.

We both do wrong and right.

And in our modern world, we are bombarded with so much conflicting advice from the 'experts':

We are told: diet, don't diet

We are told: work hard, don't work hard

We are told: love, don't love

We are told: be yourself, don't be yourself

We are told: drink red wine, don't drink red wine

We are told: eat red meat, don't eat red meat.

And so on.

But of course ultimately, the only expert in your life is you.

Life is complex. But that is its simplicity. If we understand that, we can own life.

We need to encourage children to see this. We need to talk about it and help them to live with complexity. Not to scare them, not to induce anxiety. But to prepare them for life and to help them understand what awaits them. To tell them the stories that exemplify this. We can have happy endings but children also need to hear about challenges. Fairy tales, in their original form, with their orphans, violence, evil step-mothers and shadows are a great example of literature that presents both the best and worst in life. More recently, J.K Rowling and Harry Potter have given us a whole fictional world where the extremes of emotion and experience are explored.

As a parent and an educator, I have a dual role to play in raising the next generation. Sometimes the responsibly scares me beyond belief. I worry, to misquote Philip Larkin, that I have already screwed my own children up; that my genetics have already made them anxious, over-thinking, over-sensitive: that my behaviour has already damaged them in a subtle but deep seated psychological way; that they will inevitably suffer as I have.

But I also believe deep inside that if we keep talking and allow children to understand that the world is complex, then we give them a head start in avoiding depression, anxiety and fear in years to come and in avoiding walking into a car-crash of circumstances that might lead to years of self-doubt, depression and anxiety.

Education is everything. We can't and shouldn't simplify it and talk in terms of it being the job of either teachers or parents. We need to accept that our job, as adults, is to be honest with children and to help them negotiate the complexity ahead. It is our job to develop in each child the skill to know and understand himself, the tools to express herself and the strategies to meet challenges along the way. And it is our job to talk openly and honestly so that, if and when bad things happen, like abuse, children know to talk about them so that they do not become a source of guilt, a life-stealing force, a legacy of hidden pain and shame.

Finally, we must ensure that each child has someone to trust who will listen to him or her. As the BFG says at the end of the film version of his story, each child needs someone who "hears all the secret whisperings of the world".

It is so complex and yet so simple.

Postscript

So, I wrote my book.

After she had read it, a psychologist friend suggested to me that I should maybe consider trying EMDR. This stands for Eye Movement Desensitization and Reprocessing.

As my friend is someone very wise and trustworthy, I took her suggestion on board and set about finding a therapist.

Last summer I made contact with one who offered EMDR. Living where I do, I had to look quite far afield and accepted that I would need to travel a four-hour round trip for appointments.

In our first appointment, we arranged that we would do some sessions face to face but others could be done online, which came as a great relief to me in the face of my severe carbon footprint anxiety.

At our first meeting last August we talked, explored and I left my book for her to read.

As I was leaving I noticed a book on her chair called "The Body Keeps the Score" by Bessel Van der Kolk.

She asked if I'd like to borrow it.

I said I wouldn't as I had lots of other reading on the go.

Over the next few months we met, a few times in person and a few times over an online platform. There was a lot of talking about my behaviours, my inability to relax and my obsessions, my physical compulsions. During this time I went through some exceptionally challenging times at work and I did a lot of talking about that and other distractions.

My therapist started to pick up on the fact that I would talk a lot and tactfully reflected that back to me, whilst also starting to pick up on some key themes:

My sense of blind panic at times of stress and the physical manifestation of this in my body, including holding my breath;

My constant distracting activity whether working, exercising, talking or overthinking;

My sense of worthlessness;

My values.

We talked about the fact that psychological coping mechanisms and behaviours may serve a purpose and be useful to us, when we need to cope with things that otherwise threaten to overpower us.

But we also acknowledged that coping mechanisms which are no longer needed and are actually harming us or stopping us from living a full life need to be examined and maybe challenged and stopped.

We talked about the fact that at the centre of each of us are core values and that we need to connect with those if we are to feel fulfilled.

We talked about neuroscience, the brain and the ways in which it manages our bodies, thoughts and feelings.

We talked about my past.

We talked about needing to explore my sense of worthlessness and shame.

Around Christmas I came across an old video of my final performance and assessment piece from my Dramatherapy Diploma back in 1999. I couldn't play it, as we no longer have a VCR and so I sent it off to be digitised. On watching it back, I realised that I came close, back then, to overcoming my inner demons and making peace with my history....but that something stopped me from completing the narrative and finding the "happy ever after." I reflected again on the words of my therapist back then who had said, at the end of individual therapy, that I'd done a great job but that I could not be helped any further unless I was "honest about what had hurt me" and allowed myself to "shed an ocean of tears". He knew. But he wasn't able or willing to take me to that place. Or maybe I was not ready and he knew it. I will never know.

And in January, I downloaded "The Body Keeps the Score" and read it.

I felt an absolute resonance with my experience. I can't quite put that feeling of resonance into words.

These are a couple of the parts that took my breath away:

"Traumatized people chronically feel unsafe inside their bodies: The past is alive in the form of gnawing interior discomfort. Their bodies are constantly bombarded by visceral warning signs, and, in an attempt to control these processes, they often become expert at ignoring their gut feelings and in numbing awareness of what is played out inside. They learn to hide from their selves."

"As long as you keep secrets and suppress information, you are fundamentally at war with yourself...The critical issue is allowing yourself to know what you know. That takes an enormous amount of courage."

And I realised that I needed to stop just talking.

I realised that I have been talking for ever but that the words have stopped me from really acknowledging what happened to me and has held me ransom.

In my book I wrote this:

"A memory. Aged 7. A stranger but one who had been entrusted. A violation. A child's trust betrayed. In a matter of days, everything altered. A secret held and never to be told. The beginning and the end"

But the fact is that I had not really allowed myself to process this vague memory. I had not ever spoken about it or described it in any detail. And I had not addressed the feelings and emotions that it had generated in me. I had not allowed myself to fully know what I knew.

"The Body Keeps the Score" explores therapies, processes and activities that can be helpful to those who have experienced trauma including drama (no wonder, maybe, that I have always been at my happiest when involved in plays and that I trained as a dramatherapist), yoga (which I have practised since the age of 19) and mindfulness (which I have tried, or maybe played at, with varying degrees of success). But none of these have ever quite managed to make me feel at peace or fully at one with my Self.

And then I read the section of the book about EMDR and Van Der Kolk's numerous descriptions of people for whom EMDR enabled the missing part of the jigsaw to be found.

And so, I decided that it was time to give it a go.

I won't go into detail here about the process. You can find numerous YouTube videos and articles online.

In brief, it involved spending several sessions talking about memories from my past and identifying the ones that seemed to be causing me issues. It involved building up resources that would help keep me safe while processing traumatic memories including physical positions and mental images that would enable me to connect with solidity, fierceness and nurture. It involved creating a mental image of a place where I would hold my traumatic memories while I was waiting for them to be processed; slips of paper with the memories written on in a small wooden house in the top of my wardrobe.

And then came the re-processing session.

Two hours.

Remembering.

Reliving.

Having words that I had never spoken to anyone spoken back to me describing what had happened and allowing myself to hear and feel the shame.

Shame and disgust and self-hatred pulsing through my body, my limbs.

Sobbing and sobbing and sobbing and hearing my voice sound as it did when I was a little girl, scared and shocked.

Buckets of tears and snot.

Uncontrollable feelings that were held in a safe space while my therapist worked with eye movements and then used physical, rhythmic tapping.

Other connections made with other memories and people that came as a surprise but then made sense.

Barely being able to breathe and realising that I have been holding my breath and holding my body in tension for years.

An overwhelming sense of not wanting to hold on, of wanting to collapse and be completely free of all the tension and running and blind panic.

Exhaustion.

So much physical pain in my arms, back and legs.

And all the way through, the re-assuring voice of my therapist telling me that I was doing incredibly well, holding the space for me, keeping me safe and repeating, over and over "this is the work".

And then overwhelming anger and hatred towards the person who did that to a little girl who was nothing but trusting and innocent.

And then calm.

Afterwards, a sense of it being done. Of the pieces of paper in the small wooden house being blank now.

Of needing to go to a place of nurture where I take genuine care of myself and don't just throw myself into more coping and surviving and protecting myself from something that I no longer need protection from. Of moving if I want to but more importantly of staying and stopping if I choose.

I found myself feeling sad at the end of the session and saying repeatedly that I regretted not having done this sooner; "this is what I needed. This is what was missing...." We discussed the fact that recovery often involves feelings of sadness and regret at years lost, at experiences half-lived and at energies mis-directed.

On reflection, I know that the experiences I have lived, the relationships I have formed and the contributions I have made have been meaningful and on most occasions positive and immensely valuable.

A jigsaw with a piece missing is still a jigsaw and can be colourful and beautiful and a thing of wonder. But is not complete and often it is the absent piece that will draw the eye, cause irritation and make us keep searching for that elusive piece.

I also talked at the end of the session about my fear about not having anything left at the centre, now that the layers and layers of protection have been removed and the motivation behind some of my behaviours has been challenged. What is left? How do I make decisions?

And we acknowledged that what I do have is my values and that part of what comes next may be around finding ways of ensuring that I can stay true to those.

On Sunday night I went and heard Matt Haig speak in Edinburgh. It was all that I had hoped it to be and one part of his talk in particular helped me to see that every part of my life will have had different things to offer; the person I am today is not the version of me that I was yesterday, nor the one I will be tomorrow. Staying alive is about giving the future versions of our self the chance to live and thrive and learn from the versions that have gone before.

My jigsaw is complete. If you meet me today, I am a different version of the person I was before because that irritation, that repressed anger, that constant holding of my breath and that need to fight are gone. Those tears have been cried.

My body kept a score. But now the score is settled.

Performance

My Dramatherapy final solo performance piece. Summer 1999.

Re-discovered in 2019.

(Teacher sits on a stool, doing the register).

Jason...(here)...Emily (here)...Emma...(here) and Holly..(here).

Ok Year 7, I'd like you to make yourselves comfortable and sit in position where you can sit sensibly, without talking, without fidgeting and without distracting your neighbour, because I'm going to tell you a story.

Are you sitting comfortably? Then I'll begin.

Once upon a time, there was a princess who had been captured by an evil witch and made to live on the Island of Black and White. The witch had very strict rules for this island and she spent her days reminding the princess of them and punishing her whenever she failed to obey them.

(The witch limps on, hunchbacked and with a stick. In a mean voice.)

Rule number one: you must work as hard as possible. If you do not, you are evil and deserve to be punished.

Rule number two: you must not eat too much. If you do, you are a fat pig and deserve to be punished.

Rule number three: you must not have any fun. If you do, you are wicked and deserve to be punished.

Today, as every day, you have broken every single rule on this island and deserve to be punished accordingly.

(The witch raises the stick and thrashes the princess several times).

Take that.

And that.

And that.

The princess felt very sad living on the island. More often than not, she wasn't even aware of having broken any of the rules. She felt certain that, somewhere in her past, she must have done something very, very bad...but she couldn't remember for the life of her what it was.

To make herself feel better, she would steal away when she thought the witch wasn't looking...which of course, she always was....

She would make her way to a beautiful black and white willow tree, next to a lovely black and white pond and remember the days before the island, when her life had been in colour.

Song. *Somewhere Over the Rainbow*.

The princess would often wish that the princess were dead and one day, as if by magic, her wish was granted, when a huge two storey house fell out of the sky and squashed the witch dead flat.

The princess jumped for joy and ran to her rowing boat, which the witch had made her use for fishing expeditions. She jumped in and began to row. She rowed and she rowed and she rowed...and she had no idea where she was rowing to...all she knew was that each stroke took her that bit further away from the Island of Black and White.

Imagine her disappointment when she arrived on a distant shore to find that it too was in black and white. She looked around her; this new land was full of beautiful trees and ponds and buildings but no-where was there a flash of colour to be seen. At that moment, the princess vowed that her mission, from then on, would be to find the colours of the rainbow and to bring them back into the world around her.

She wandered around for some time, until she came to a room full of people. Amazingly, all of these people seemed to have similar issues to her own. They chatted and exchanged ideas and from then on, they met up at regular intervals over a period of many years. Together, they experienced all sorts of opportunities which were new and exciting to the princess, such as "Peer Group Facilitation", "Ritual Transformation" and one occasion of " Para-theatrical Activity"!!

The princess faced many challenges along the way.

"Ah, yes, I've asked for this meeting as I was wondering whether it might be possible for me to extend my overdraft limit? Um, three thousand pounds?"

"Yeah, um, I know it says something different in the course handbook, um but I was wondering whether I could do my individual therapy before my group therapy because I'm not very good with groups?"

"For God's sake, I've been doing it for a year now, I've learnt all these structures and not ONE of them is actually suitable for the client group I'm working with!!"

"I can't do it. I've got no ideas whatsoever, I've got no time to plan it and there is NO WAY I'm going to be able to stand for 15 minutes on that stage by myself!"

The princess faced and met the many challenges and she was very pleased that along her journey, she began to see sparks of colour beginning to come back into the world around her.

But as she approached the end of the path, she began to question what she might have to do to bring ALL the colours of the rainbow back into her life.

As she asked herself this question, she felt drawn to return to the place where she had spent so long trying to get out of her despair and desperation. Back to the Island of Black and White.

She jumped into her rowing boat and began to row and row and row.

Once there, she made her way to the beautiful black and white willow, next to the lovely black and white pond.

She looked down and asked the question: "Where can I find the colours of the rainbow?"

And as I looked down, I saw my face reflected in the water below and I know that I had found the answer.

Red is the colour of my anger.

Orange is the colour of the flames of my energy.

Yellow is the sunshine of my laughter.

Green is the calmness of my soul.

Blue is the sadness of my tears.

And purple is my passion.

Song -*True Colours.*

Inspirations and sources

DBC Pierre, author, speaking on Radio 4's 'Open Book' 28th July 2016.

Brené Brown, Listening To Shame, TED Talk, March 2012

at https://www.ted.com/talks/brene_brown_listening_to_shame?language=en

Reasons to Stay Alive. Matt Haig. Canongate Books, 2015.

(Extract used with kind permission of Canongate.)

Inner Story: Understand your Mind. Change your World. Dr Tim O'Brien. Kindle Books, 2015.

(Extract used with kind permission of Dr Tim O' Brien).

Letting Go: How to Heal Your Hurt, Love Your Body and Transform Your Life. Emma Woolf. Summersdale. 2015.

(Extract used with kind permission of Emma Woolf).

Harry Potter and the Cursed Child. JK Rowling, John Tiffany and Jack Thorne. Little, Brown Book Group, 2016. Harry Potter Publishing and Theatrical rights © J.K. Rowling 2016.

(Extract used with kind permission of The Blair Partnership).

The Body Keeps The Score: Mind, Brain and Body in the Transformation of Trauma. Bessel van der Kolk. Penguin. 24 September 2015.

(Extract used with kind permission of Bessel Van der Kolk).

Printed in Great Britain
by Amazon